NOT INCONSIDERABLE...

Being the life and times of John Major

BY THE SAME AUTHOR

101 Uses for a John Major
101 Further Uses for a John Major

NOT INCONSIDERABLE...

Being the life and times of John Major

PATRICK WRIGHT

ANDRE DEUTSCH

First published in Great Britain in 1996 by
André Deutsch Limited
106 Great Russell Street
London WC1B 3LJ

Cataloguing-in-Publication data available for this title
from the British Library

ISBN 0 233 98958 7

Printed in Great Britain by
WBC, Bridgend

For Frances, Joe and Amy

Acknowledgements

Many thanks to Simon Hoggart, whose speculations on the origins of the Prime Minister's unique manner of speaking have been the inspiration for the part of this book dealing with Major's time in Nigeria. I should also thank him for supplying detailed notes and a chronology of the many calamitous events which have bedevilled this Government since 1992. I'm only sorry there has not been room in this book to use them all.

Especial thanks to Marguerite Millar, without whose skills with the word processor and cheery disposition this book would never have been delivered to the publisher. Oh no.

Acknowledgement should also be given to: Penny Junor, *The Major Enigma* (Michael Joseph, 1994); Terry Major-Ball, *Major, Major* (Duckworth, 1994); Linda Lee-Potter, Interview with Jean Collins, *Mail on Sunday* and *Daily Mail,* February 1995; Cassandra Jardine, Interview with Patricia Dessoy (née Major), *Daily Telegraph,* June 1996.

Foreword

Sometime during the summer of 1994, while rootling through a box of junk at a local car-boot sale, I chanced upon two books. The first was Penny Junor's *The Major Enigma,* and the second was *Major, Major* by the Prime Minister's brother, Terry. Both books bore the inscription 'To Gerald, with the earnest wish that you soon overcome your infatuation with Messrs. Blair and Ashdown and return to "fold". With much love from Aunt Maude.' The photographs in both had been mutilated, and profanities had been scrawled in the margins of almost every page.

What, I wondered, could these two seemingly innocuous items possibly contain to produce such a violent reaction in their recipient? I decided to buy them.

'How much do you want for those books Aunt Maude gave you, darling?' the woman behind the stall inquired of an ill-tempered looking man sitting nearby.

'I thought I told you to burn the bloody things,' the man said somewhat tetchily.

'Just because you've been made redundant, there's no need to adopt that tone with me,' the woman snapped back.

I sensed an unpleasant atmosphere was beginning to develop between these two, and cautiously offered a ten-pence piece for the books which was snatched from my hand with an alarming zeal.

Back home, I settled down and began to browse through my two purchases. Within minutes I was in deep sleep.

As I slept, my dreams were beset by images of gnomes and rabbits. Bananas and underpants. Images of a child, born into a wildly eccentric family of former circus performers turned garden gnome manufacturers who, despite this obvious advantage, resolved at an early age to turn his back on the hopelessly failing family business in order to climb the greasy pole of British Politics only to find that, regardless of his best efforts, he was destined to remain the most famous maker of garden gnomes in the history of the world. Truly, I thought upon waking, this man is an enigma. Oh yes.

For several months I pondered on the conundrum that is John Major until one day I determined to write and illustrate my own biography of this extraordinary Englishman.

On the same day, I realised I had mislaid both the books I'd bought at the car-boot sale and that I would be obliged to produce this book largely from the memory of what I had read some months previously. So, while I'm fairly sure the incidents and events depicted here are based in fact, I have had to employ a certain amount of conjecture in the detail. Oh well.

Since I completed this book it has been suggested that certain parts of it may prove offensive to some, whereas others may find 'political incorrectness' exactly where it is intended. Sorry about that. It has been my intention throughout to be even-handed in an effort to affront as many people as possible. In some places the names have been changed to protect the innocent.

NOT INCONSIDERABLE ...

Being the life and times of John Major

MARCH 29th 1943 AND NAZI BOMBERS DROP THEIR DEADLY CARGO OVER LONDON.

INSIDE NUMBER 260 LONGFELLOW ROAD, TIM AND GWEN MAJOR WERE MORE CONCERNED WITH GWEN'S DIGESTION THAN WITH NAZI BOMBS.

BUT GWEN MAJOR DIDN'T HAVE INDIGESTION; SHE WAS PREGNANT. WITHIN SECONDS SHE GAVE BIRTH TO A BABY BOY.

SOON THOUGH, THE WAR INTERRUPTED THE MAJORS' RUSTIC IDYLL, AND OLD TOM WAS CALLED TO SERVE WITH THE UNITED STATES AIR FORCE.

FOR KING AND COUNTRY THE MAJORS DO THEIR BIT. OH YES.

LITTLE IS KNOWN OF TOM'S EXPLOITS AS A PILOT BUT HIS ACROBATIC SKILLS MUST HAVE IMPRESSED HIS FELLOW AIRMEN, AND WOULD CERTAINLY HAVE CONFOUNDED THE LUFTWAFFE'S FINEST AIR ACES.

DONNER UND BLITZEN!

JEEZE! THAT OLD GUY'S SURE GOT BALLS.

WITH TOM AWAY, GWEN WAS LEFT TO CARE FOR HER YOUNG SON. IT WAS NOT AN EASY TIME; FOOD WAS IN SHORT SUPPLY, AND IN DESPERATION GWEN TURNED TO A LOCAL PIG FARMER WHO KINDLY ALLOWED HER TO FEED JOHN ON THE SWILL MEANT FOR HIS PIGS. THIS EXPERIENCE PROBABLY ACCOUNTS FOR JOHN MAJOR'S PREFERENCE FOR MOTORWAY SERVICE STATION FOOD.

THAT'S IT, LADDY. YOUSE GET STUCK IN.

YOU'RE VERY KIND, MISTER.

SLURP GOBBLE MMM

DURING THE LONG SUMMER MONTHS OF 1944, GWEN WOULD SPEND HOURS WALKING THROUGH THE NORFOLK COUNTRYSIDE WITH THE INFANT JOHN. IT WAS ON ONE OF THESE WALKS THAT JOHN SAW HIS FIRST RABBITS: IT WAS TO LEAVE AN INDELIBLE IMPRESSION ON HIM.

LOOK JOHN. BUNNY RABBITS.

AS THE WAR DREW TO AN END, TOM DECIDED IT WAS SAFE FOR HIS FAMILY TO RETURN TO LONDON. SO, IN APRIL 1945, THEY BADE FAREWELL TO THEIR MANY FRIENDS. IT WAS AN EMOTIONAL OCCASION.

WAH! THEY'RE TAKING THE GREY ONE FROM US!

DON'T GO!

MANY HOURS LATER THE MAJORS ARRIVED BACK IN LONGFELLOW ROAD.

CRIKEY DUCKS! IN NO SMALL MEASURE IT'S GOOD TO SEE THE OLD HOUSE AGAIN.

ALTHOUGH THE WAR WAS OVER, BRITAIN WAS PLUNGED INTO AN ERA OF GREAT AUSTERITY. POVERTY WAS RIFE IN LONGFELLOW ROAD. AND GWEN - WHO HAD A SOFT SPOT FOR ANYONE DOWN ON THEIR LUCK - TURNED THE TINY BUNGALOW INTO A REFUGE FOR THE NEEDY. WORD OF HER PHILANTHROPY QUICKLY SPREAD, AND SOON THE LITTLE HOUSE WAS OVER-RUN BY POVERTY-STRICKEN STRANGERS FROM ALL OVER THE COUNTRY. THE YOUNG JOHN WAS DAILY ENCOURAGED TO GIVE UP HIS OWN MEAGRE PORTIONS TO THESE PEOPLE.

GOOD MORNING, DEAR LADY. MAY I BEG A CUP OF TEA? PERHAPS ... ER SOMETHING A LITTLE STRONGER? THROAT'S A BIT DRY.

HAND OVER THAT CRUMPET, YOU LITTLE GREY BLEEDER, OR I'LL GIVE YOU A RIGHT LARRUPIN!

OH, YOU POOR MAN!

ANOTHER CRUMPET WHEN YOU'RE READY MISSUS.

BEFORE THE WAR, TOM MAJOR HAD OWNED A HIGHLY SUCCESSFUL BUSINESS MANUFACTURING CONCRETE GNOMES. TOM WAS A STAUNCH TORY, AND HE LOOKED FORWARD TO REVIVING HIS BUSINESS'S FORTUNES UNDER A CONSERVATIVE GOVERNMENT NOW THE WAR WAS OVER.

HOWEVER, TOM'S CONFIDENCE IN A BRIGHT FUTURE WAS QUICKLY DASHED WHEN AN UNGRATEFUL NATION REJECTED THE CONSERVATIVES AND VOTED IN A LABOUR GOVERNMENT UNDER CLEMENT ATTLEE. TOM MAJOR TOOK THE RESULT BADLY.

BASTARDS! A NATION OF UNGRATEFUL BASTARDS!

CALM DOWN, DEAREST.

BASTARDS?

DEEPLY DEPRESSED, TOM DEVELOPED A SIEGE MENTALITY.

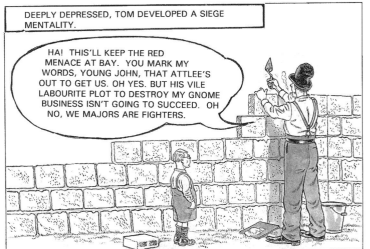

HA! THIS'LL KEEP THE RED MENACE AT BAY. YOU MARK MY WORDS, YOUNG JOHN, THAT ATTLEE'S OUT TO GET US. OH YES. BUT HIS VILE LABOURITE PLOT TO DESTROY MY GNOME BUSINESS ISN'T GOING TO SUCCEED. OH NO, WE MAJORS ARE FIGHTERS.

HAVING BUILT THE HUGE BREEZE-BLOCK WALL TO PROTECT HIS FAMILY AGAINST MARAUDING SOCIALISTS, TOM TURNED HIS ATTENTIONS TO THE GARDEN.

SHALLOTS. WE'LL PLANT ENOUGH SHALLOTS TO KEEP US GOING UNTIL A TORY GOVERNMENT IS RETURNED AT THE NEXT ELECTION.

IN NO TIME THE LITTLE GARDEN AT 260 LONGFELLOW ROAD WAS KNEE HIGH IN SHALLOTS.

I'LL GET YOU SOME KILNER JARS, THEN YOU CAN SET TO AND PICKLE THIS LOT.

I'VE GOT A LOVELY RECIPE IN MY GOOD HOUSEKEEPING COOKBOOK - SHALLOTS AVEC SHALLOTS. IT'S FRENCH, I THINK.

OLD TOM WAS A STAUNCH CONSERVATIVE, AND HE AND GWEN WOULD FREQUENTLY ENTERTAIN THEIR LOCAL MP ON THESE OCCASIONS - POOR THOUGH THEY WERE - NO EXPENSE WAS SPARED.

HOPE YOU LIKE OUR TEA SERVICE, IT'S OUR BEST. SPODE, MY LORD.

PERHAPS YOU'D LIKE SOMETHING A LITTLE STRONGER? SCOTCH MAYBE? GO DOWN PERFECT WITH THE SHALLOT SARNY.

SO IT IS, DEAR LADY. SPODE. MMM.

THE INFANT JOHN WOULD SIT ENTHRALLED AS OLD TOM DISCUSSED THE POLITICAL ISSUES OF THE DAY WITH HIS IMPORTANT GUEST.

I TELL YOU, SIR. IF I EVER GET MY 'ANDS ON THAT ATTLEE, I'LL FLAY THE SKIN FROM HIS BACK. THEN I'D CUT OFF HIS PRIVATES AND SHOVE 'EM UP HIS JACKSY. AND THEN I'D SLICE ...

QUITE SO. WHA...? 'NUTHER SCOTCH? DON'T MIND IF I DO.

TOM'S POLITICAL AFFILIATION AND OPINIONS WERE WELL KNOWN TO THE LARGELY SOCIALIST COMMUNITY IN WORCESTER PARK. SOME WENT OUT OF THEIR WAY TO ANTAGONISE THE OLD MAN.

YOU TORY BASTARD - IT'S OUR TURN NOW.

A LABOURITE! A BLOODY LABOURITE WALKING IN FRONT OF <u>MY</u> HOUSE!

THE NEXT PAGE IS QUITE EXCITING ...

ANOTHER INGENIOUS GAME THE YOUNGSTER INVENTED BECAME INTERNATIONALLY KNOWN AS 'ONE MAN CRICKET'. AGAIN, JOHN MAJOR WOULD PLAY THIS GAME WITH A SINGLE-MINDEDNESS THAT WOULD SERVE HIM WELL IN LATER LIFE.

HOWEVER, THE GAME WAS NOT WITHOUT ITS HAZARDS ...

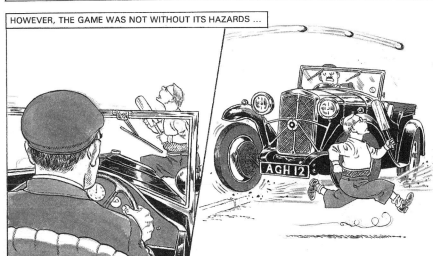

... AND SOON THIS ACTIVITY, TOO, HAD TO BE CURTAILED.

BY THE TIME HE WAS SIX, JOHN MAJOR WAS BEGINNING TO DISPLAY A REMARKABLE GRASP OF CAPITALISM AND ECONOMICS - A COMPREHENSION THAT WAS LATER TO DESERT HIM. JOHN BY NOW OWNED AN ANGORAN DOE RABBIT AND SOME RATS, WHILE A NEIGH-BOURING FRIEND OWNED A BEVAN BUCK RABBIT. THE TWO BOYS RESOLVED TO BREED FROM THESE CREATURES AND THEN TO SELL THE ENSUING OFF-SPRING TO RABBIT FANCIERS AND THE STARVING.

LOOK, JOHN, THEY'RE SHAGGIN'.

SOON THEY HAD ENOUGH RABBITS AND RATS TO GO INTO BUSINESS. THE TWO BOYS SET UP THEIR STALL ON THE PAVEMENT OUTSIDE JOHN'S HOME.

MUNY BOCS

RABITS AND RATS Big mice FOUR SAIL RABITS 2/6 (7/6 four too) Big mice 6p

UNFORTUNATELY, NEITHER BOY HAD HEARD THE EXPRESSION 'TO BREED LIKE RABBITS', AND SOON THEY HAD MORE RABBITS AND RATS THAN THEY COULD SELL, OR EVEN CONTAIN.

RABBITS! RATS! COME AND GET 'EM WHILE STOCKS LAST! SALE NOW ON! BUY TWO AND GET A PIECE OF JOHN'S MUM'S CAKE FREE.

AAARGH! RATS!

REGRETTABLY, THE ENTERPRISE GOT OUT OF HAND AS WORCESTER PARK BECAME OVERRUN BY THE CREATURES AND THE COUNCIL'S PEST CONTROL DEPARTMENT WAS CALLED IN.

JOHN HAD OFTEN OVERHEARD HIS PARENTS DISCUSSING THE GNOME BUSINESS AND SOMETHING CALLED A 'TERRY', ALTHOUGH HE HAD NO IDEA WHAT THIS LATTER MIGHT BE.

... MUMBLE, MUMBLE ... TIME THE LITTLE GREY BUGGER ... MUMBLE ... TERRY ... MUMBLE ...

BY NOW JOHN HAD PERSUADED HIS FATHER TO LET HIM HAVE A DOG - AFFECTIONATELY NAMED 'THE BUTCHER'. THE BUTCHER WOULD SNUGGLE UP IN BED WITH YOUNG JOHN WHILE HE BROODED ON THE MEANING OF A 'TERRY' (THE YOUNG JOHN, THAT IS. NOT THE DOG).

TERRY? TE-REE?

GRRRRR. SNARL.

JOHN HAD DEVELOPED AN ESPECIAL FONDNESS FOR ALL CREATURES GREAT AND SMALL. ON ONE OCCASION HE PUT BARRIER CREAM ON THE GOLDFISH TO PROTECT THEM FROM THE SUN'S RAYS. IN THIS WAY, MANY GOLD-FISH WERE SAVED FROM CARCINOGENIC SCALE DISEASE.

THEN, ONE DAY - WHEN THE YOUNG JOHN WAS ADMINISTERING A PAIN KILLER TO A STRICKEN ANIMAL IN THE GARDEN - HIS FATHER CAME TO HIM.

YOUR MOTHER TELLS ME YOU MIGHT BE SIX OR SEVEN YEARS OLD NOW*. I THINK IT MIGHT BE AN IDEA TO HAVE A LITTLE CHAT.

THE MAJORS WERE SO POOR THAT THEY DIDN'T CELEBRATE JOHN'S BIRTHDAY, AND CONSEQUENTLY NEVER KNEW EXACTLY HOW OLD HE WAS. JOHN HIMSELF IS CONFUSED ON THIS MATTER, CLAIMING TO HAVE BEEN SAVED AT BIRTH BY THE NHS, DESPITE BEING BORN THREE YEARS BEFORE ITS INTRODUCTION.

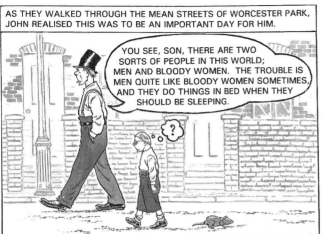

AS THEY WALKED THROUGH THE MEAN STREETS OF WORCESTER PARK, JOHN REALISED THIS WAS TO BE AN IMPORTANT DAY FOR HIM.

YOU SEE, SON, THERE ARE TWO SORTS OF PEOPLE IN THIS WORLD; MEN AND BLOODY WOMEN. THE TROUBLE IS MEN QUITE LIKE BLOODY WOMEN SOMETIMES, AND THEY DO THINGS IN BED WHEN THEY SHOULD BE SLEEPING.

THIS WAS A REVELATION TO THE YOUNG CHILD.

THAT'S HOW YOU CAME INTO THIS BLOODY, BUGGERING LABOURITE TOILET OF A WORLD. SO, WHATEVER ELSE YOU DO IN LIFE, MAKE SURE NO BASTARD INTERRUPTS YOUR KIP. DO I MAKE MYSELF CLEAR?

OH, YES.

TOS' MAJOR
OME FACTORY
BY APPOINTMENT

LABOURITES KEEP OUT!

REVELATION FOLLOWED REVELATION.

TORY
MENT

LABOURIT
KEEPOU

ANYWAY, LONG BEFORE YOU WERE BORN, YOUR MUM AND ME HAD ANOTHER BAD NIGHT'S SLEEP - TWO IN FACT.

TAKING A HUGE, RUSTY KEY FROM HIS POCKET, THE OLD MAN UNLOCKED THE DOOR TO MAJOR'S GNOMES FACTORY.

INSIDE, THE YOUNG BOY PEERED INTO THE GLOOM. AT THE END OF THE BUILDING HE COULD MAKE OUT ALMOST FAMILIAR SHAPES. HOWEVER, ONE OF THESE SHAPES WAS DECIDEDLY UNFAMILIAR.

TE-REE? WHERE ARE YOU, BOY?

THE UNFAMILIAR FORM BEGAN TO SHUFFLE TOWARD THEM. INSTINCTIVELY, THE YOUNG BOY RECOILED FROM THE APPARITION.

I'M HERE, DAD.

DAD?

JOHN LISTENED SPELL-BOUND AS HIS FATHER SPOKE WITH 'THE TE-REE'.

I'M RUNNING SHORT OF CEMENT, DAD. HAVING TO USE FOUR-AND-A-HALF SAND TO HALF OF CEMENT. THE GNOMES ARE FALLING APART. AND THE ZINC RIDDLE'S GOT HOLES IN IT!

IT'S SUPPOSED TO, TERRY. LOOK, I NEED TWENTY MODEL 14 GNOMES BY THE MORNING; I'VE GOT A BUNCH OF BANANAS COMING IN AT ELEVEN. AND, NO GNOMES, NO BANANAS. GOT IT?

TOM WOULD OFTEN SWAP A SMALL QUANTITY OF GNOMES FOR BANANAS.

FINALLY, TOM INTRODUCED JOHN TO HIS OLDER (AND DESTINED TO BECOME MORE FAMOUS) BROTHER.

ANYWAY. JOHN, THIS IS OUR TERRY. HE'S YOUR BROTHER. OH, AND BY THE WAY, YOU'VE GOT A SISTER CALLED ... ER ... PAT'. THAT'S RIGHT ISN'T IT TERRY?

THAT'S RIGHT, DAD.

ONE DAY ALL THIS WILL BE YOURS SON.

OH, NO.

WHAT ABOUT ME, DAD?

THAT NIGHT, WHILE HE SNUGGLED UP TO 'THE BUTCHER', JOHN RESOLVED NEVER TO GO INTO THE GNOME BUSINESS. INSTEAD, HIS THOUGHTS TURNED TO HIS FATHER'S FRIEND - THE KINDLY TORY M.P.

GNOMES! GNOMES! OH NO! NO!

MY DEAR, DEAR BOY.

I WUNT TO BE LIKE THAT NICE MAN DAD TALKS AT. THEN I CAN GO TO LOTS OF PEOPLE'S HOUSES AND HAVE TEA AND FOOD.

VERY LITTLE IS KNOWN OF JOHN'S SCHOOLDAYS. HE WAS A POPULAR BOY BECAUSE HE NEVER ARGUED WITH THE OTHER BOYS.

WELL, MAJOR. WHAT IS IT?

WELL, ON THE ONE HAND ... AND THEN ON THE OTHER ... IT MIGHT JUST BE ... BUT THEN MAYBE NOT ...

CRIKEY, JOHN! MAKE YOUR MIND UP; IS IT HEADS OR IS IT TAILS?

JOHN HAS ALWAYS BEEN KEEN ON FOOTBALL. HOWEVER, THE TWO MAIN SPORTS AT HIS SCHOOL WERE RUGBY AND CRICKET. IT WAS FRUSTRATING FOR HIM TO FIND THAT THE FOOTBALL WAS THE WRONG SHAPE ...

REF'. FOUL! HE'S CARRYING THE BALL!

... AND THAT CRICKET WAS A TEAM GAME PLAYED ONLY DURING THE SUMMER TERM.

BY THE EARLY 1950'S TOM MAJOR'S GNOME BUSINESS WAS GOING INTO DECLINE. THE MOULDS USED TO MANUFACTURE THE GNOMES WERE SO WORN THAT THEY PRODUCED ONLY HORRIBLE LUMPS OF CONCRETE WHICH TERRY WOULD HAVE TO SCULPT INTO SOME SORT OF RECOGNISABLE SHAPE.

GO AND WASH YOUR BLOODY MOUTH OUT.

OH, BUGGER!

THINGS WENT FROM BAD TO WORSE.

'MORNING, TERRY. WELL, DID YOU GET THAT BIG ORDER FOR BENTALLS COMPLETED DURING THE NIGHT?

SORT OF.

TERRY. HOW MANY GNOMES DID BENTALLS NEED BY THIS MORNING?

THIRTY, DAD.

AND HOW MANY GNOMES CAN I SEE HERE, TERRY?

ONE AND A HALF, DAD.

THAT'S RIGHT, SON. ONE AND A HALF GNOMES. YOU CALL THAT A NIGHT'S WORK?

I CAN'T COPE, DAD.. I HAVEN'T SEEN DAYLIGHT IN MONTHS. I CAN'T SLEEP. AND THE GNOMES ARE TALKING ABOUT ME BEHIND MY BACK!

THEN, ONE DAY, A WEALTHY WIDOW AND HER GENTLEMAN FRIEND ARRIVED AT THE GNOME FACTORY WITH AN OFFER TOM COULDN'T REFUSE.

DAD, THERE'S A LADY HERE WHO WANTS TO BUY THE BUSINESS.

WELCOME! WELCOME, DEAR LADY.

IT SEEMED LIKE THE ANSWER TO ALL TOM'S PROBLEMS.

OH, MY LOVELY MONEY - I MEAN LADY. THREE THOUSAND QUID AND IT'S YOURS. AND I'LL THROW TERRY IN AS A GESTURE OF GOODWILL.

TOM HAD AN OLD- FASHIONED ATTITUDE TO BUSINESS DEALS.

I'LL GET MY SOLICITOR TO DRAW UP THE NECESSARY DOCUMENTS, MR. MAJOR.

?

NO NEED FOR ALL THAT PAPERWORK, LADY. YOU JUST GIVE ME £3000, WE SHAKE HANDS, AND - BOB'S YOUR UNCLE - YOU'VE GOT A GNOME BUSINESS.

THE DEAL WAS DONE.

AS YOU WISH. HERE YOU ARE - £3000.

TA!

HOWEVER, THE DEAL WAS NOT AS SIMPLE AS TOM HAD HOPED.

YOU SEE, MR. MAJOR, I'M MOST ANXIOUS THAT MY ... ER ... FRIEND, EUSTACE, SHOULD FIND GAINFUL EMPLOYMENT. I HEARD YOUR BUSINESS WAS IN NEED OF A LITTLE CAPITAL, AND FELT THIS MIGHT BE A GOLDEN OPPORTUNITY FOR EUSTACE TO LEARN ALL ABOUT GARDEN GNOMES.

YEAH? TWO THOUSAND ONE HUNDRED. A GOLDEN OPPORTUNITY. TWO THOUSAND TWO HUNDRED. TERRY'LL LEARN HIM.

THE LITTLE BUNGALOW IN LONGFELLOW ROAD WAS EVENTUALLY SOLD AND THE PROCEEDS USED TO REPAY THE WIDOW. ALTHOUGH OLD TOM WAS NOW EFFECTIVELY BROKE HE BORE THE WIDOW NO ILL WILL.

WELL, REALLY ...!

HERE'S YOUR BLOODY MONEY, YOU VICE-RIDDEN OLD BAG. I HOPE YOU GET THE SQUITS EVERY DAY FOR THE REST OF YOUR LIFE. NOW SOD OFF!

AND SO TOM AND HIS FAMILY MOVED TO A RUN-DOWN PART OF BRIXTON.

BLIMEY, GWEN. TERRY'LL REALLY HAVE TO GET HIS FINGER OUT TO PRODUCE ENOUGH GNOMES TO GET US OUT OF THIS DUMP.

THEIR NEW LODGINGS CONSISTED OF TWO SHABBY ROOMS AT THE TOP OF A RUN-DOWN HOUSE ON THE CORNER OF COLDHARBOUR LANE. THE REST OF THE HOUSE WAS OCCUPIED BY AN ODD ASSORTMENT OF FOLK.

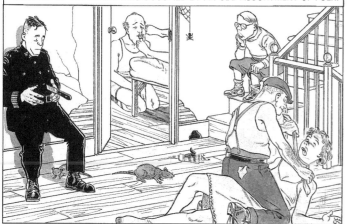

ONCE AGAIN, GWEN MADE THE LITTLE ROOMS A HAVEN FOR ALL THE LAME DUCKS IN THE AREA. OFTEN SHE WOULD SCRAMBLE ONE EGG FOR AS MANY AS A DOZEN PEOPLE.

NOW DON'T EAT IT ALL AT ONCE.

DON'T SUPPOSE YOU'VE A LITTLE BREAD TO PUT IT ON, MISSUS? MAKE IT STRETCH A BIT FURTHER, LIKE. PIECE OF CARDBOARD WOULD DO.

THE MAJORS WERE OBLIGED TO SHARE A BATHROOM TWO FLOORS DOWN WITH THE OTHER RESIDENTS OF 144 COLDHARBOUR LANE.

OUT OF THE WAY, MISTER, THE GREY ONE'S ABOUT TO DO HIS KAKA!

NOT AGAIN! THE LITTLE BUGGER MUST BE FULL OF THE STUFF!

BATHTIME WAS ALSO DIFFICULT.

WHERE'S ME RUBBER DUCK?

GIVE US THE SOAP BEFORE I KILL YOU.

DON'T PEE IN THE BATH, SON; IT'S BAD FORM.

ALTHOUGH, BY NOW, JOHN WAS THIRTEEN YEARS OLD, GWEN - A NATURALLY DOTING MOTHER - INSISTED THAT HIS BOWEL MOVEMENTS WERE REGULAR.

COME ON POPPIT. SQUEEZE. OTHERWISE IT'LL ALL BUILD UP AND YOU'LL EXPLODE.

YEAH, COME ON, SON; I NEEDS A WIDDLE.

GWEN'S INSISTENCE WOULD RETURN TO HAUNT JOHN IN LATER YEARS.

RAT-INFESTED HOVEL THOUGH IT WAS, TOM WAS SOON ENTERTAINING FRIENDS FROM HIS VAUDEVILLE DAYS.

LARRY, DEAR BOY.

IT'S CALLED THE 'WOOING OF TARZAN'.

NO, TOM, IT'S LIZ.

ABSOLUTELY SCINTILLATING, DEAR LADY.

JOHN WOULD NEVER FORGET HIS MOTHER'S 'WOOING OF TARZAN' ROUTINE, AND WAS TO USE IT TO GREAT EFFECT IN LATER YEARS.

DESPITE THE ATTENTIONS OF OLD FRIENDS FROM HIS THEATRICAL DAYS, OLD TOM'S HEALTH WAS FAILING, AND HE COULD DO LITTLE TO HELP TERRY AT THE GNOME FACTORY. HOWEVER, HE REMAINED UNWILLING TO RELINQUISH CONTROL OF THE BUSINESS, AND HIS INSTRUCTIONS BECAME INCREASINGLY IMPERIOUS AND ECCENTRIC.

I WANT HUGE GNOMES. MONUMENTAL GNOMES! CAST IN BRONZE.

BUT GNOMES ARE SUPPOSED TO BE SMALLISH THINGS, DAD.

WELL, PERHAPS YOU COULD MAKE YOUR OLD DAD A SMALLISH MONUMENTAL GNOME.

MEANWHILE JOHN CONTINUED TO STRUGGLE WITH HIS EDUCATION WITHIN AN INSTITUTION HE INCREASINGLY HATED DUE TO THE WEAK HEADSHIP OF A MR. BLENKINSOP NICKNAMED CHAMPION THE WONDER HORSE BECAUSE OF HIS HUGE TEETH.

... ER ... GET ON AND DO WHATEVER IT IS ... ER ... BOYS DO IN LESSONS ... MMM ... YES, THAT'S IT. I'LL POP BACK AT THE END OF THE DAY TO ... ER ... SEE ALL IS TICKETY-BOO.

ANOTHER TEACHER ADMINISTERED THE ONLY BEATING JOHN RECEIVED AT THE SCHOOL, ALTHOUGH HE WOULD RECEIVE MORE SEVERE BEATINGS MUCH LATER IN HIS LIFE.

THIS IS GOING TO HURT ME MORE THAN IT IS YOU, MAJOR. NOW, WHATEVER YOU DO YOU MUSN'T TURN ROUND AND LOOK AT ME WHILE I'M DOING THIS.

JOHN VEGETATED AT SCHOOL. HE HATED MATHS, SCIENCE, ENGLISH, GEOGRAPHY, DIVINITY, AND HE DETERMINED TO LEAVE THE MOMENT HE TURNED SIXTEEN, ALTHOUGH, OF COURSE, HE WASN'T SURE WHEN THIS MIGHT BE.

IN THE EVENT, JOHN LEFT SCHOOL SOMETIME DURING 1959. EXACTLY HOW MANY QUALIFICATIONS HE ATTAINED AT THE END OF HIS FORMAL EDUCATION REMAINS A MATTER OF SOME CONJECTURE. HOWEVER, HE APPLIED HIMSELF TO THE TASK OF GAINING EMPLOYMENT WITH ENTHUSIASM.

BUGGER OFF.

HELLO, SIR. FOR A NOT INCONSIDERABLE PERIOD OF TIME IT HAS BEEN MY AMBITION TO BE A BUS CONDUCTOR; A JOB WHICH, IN MY JUDGEMENT, I AM MORE THAN QUALIFIED FOR. PLEASE ALLOW ME TO DEMONSTRATE MY TECHNIQUE: ALL ABOARD - DING DING.

JOHN RECEIVED SEVERAL SUCH REJECTIONS. THEN HE LANDED A JOB SHUFFLING PAPER FOR A FIRM OF CITY BROKERS. HE HATED IT, FEELING OUT OF PLACE IN THE SMART ENVIRONMENT, AND AWKWARD IN THE ILL-FITTING SUIT HE'D BOUGHT HIMSELF. QUITE WHY HE BOUGHT A SUIT THAT DIDN'T FIT REMAINS PART OF THE ENIGMA THAT IS JOHN MAJOR.

SHALL I SHUFFLE THESE PAPERS NOW?

WHAT? OH YES, SHUFFLE AWAY, BOY. TRY AND MAKE SURE THE PAPERS IN THE MIDDLE ARE SHUFFLED TO THE FRONT AND BACK, AND THOSE AT THE FRONT AND BACK ARE SHUFFLED TO THE MIDDLE. GAD, MAJOR, YOU MUST INTRODUCE ME TO YOUR TAILOR, HAW, HAW.

MEANWHILE, CHANGES WERE AFOOT AT MAJOR'S GNOME FACTORY. A KINDLY NAVAL COMMANDER HAD BOUGHT THE FIRM AND SOON THE MAJORS WERE FINANCIALLY SECURE AGAIN. HOWEVER, TERRY NEEDED AN EXTRA PAIR OF HANDS.

I NEED AN EXTRA PAIR OF HANDS, JOHN. OF COURSE, I'D NEED ARMS AS WELL, AND MY OVERALLS WOULD NEED TO BE ALTERED ACCORDINGLY...

WHAT ARE YOU TRYING TO TELL ME, TERRY?

AND I'LL TELL YOU THIS, LITTLE BROTHER. THE LADIES REALLY GO FOR A CHAP WHO CAN TURN OUT A SELVAGE-FREE GNOME.

I'M TALKING GNOMES, JOHN. THERE'S A LOT OF MONEY IN THAT GREY POWDER. IT'S THE 'FUTURE'. WHY DON'T YOU JOIN ME IN THE 'FUTURE', JOHN.

RELUCTANTLY, JOHN AGREED TO JOIN HIS BROTHER AT THE GNOME FACTORY.

THOSE GNOMES NEED DISTRESSING JOHN.

WHAT DO I SAY TO DISTRESS THEM TERRY?

MANGANESE DIOXIDE.

DON'T THEY LIKE THOSE WORDS, THEN, TERRY?

DEAR GOD, JOHN. YOU PAINT THEM WITH THE STUFF AND THAT DISTRESSES THEM.

ISN'T THAT A BIT CRUEL, TERRY?

AUTHOR'S NOTE: CLEARLY, THIS SCENE COULD GO ON FOREVER, BUT WE MUST MOVE ON.

WITH THEIR FORTUNES NOW IMPROVED, THE MAJORS WERE AT LAST ABLE TO LEAVE THE SQUALOR OF COLDHARBOUR LANE. AND SO, LATE IN 1959, THEY MOVED TO MORE SPACIOUS PREMISES AT 80 BURTON ROAD. THEIR ARRIVAL DID NOT GO UNNOTICED.

OOH! I LIKE THE LOOK OF HIM. A BIT GREY, BUT G-O-R-G-E-O-U-S!

SHORTLY AFTER THEY MOVED, THERE CAME A KNOCK ON THE DOOR.

HELLO, I'M SORRY, I'LL GO AWAY ... PLEASE FORGIVE ME AND DON'T HIT ME. I KNOW I'M HORRIBLE AND EVERYBODY HATES ME. I'LL JUST GO AWAY AND KILL MYSELF.

BUT WHAT IS IT YOU WANT?

DO YOU REALLY WANT TO KNOW? WELL, I BELONG TO THE YOUNG CONSERVATIVES, AND - AS A PUNISHMENT - THEY'VE SENT ME OUT TO RECRUIT NEW MEMBERS.

BUT WE DO HAVE LOTS OF JOLLY GOOD FUN AT THE Y.C.s. WE HAVE WHIST DRIVES, APPLEBOBBING AND FIND THE 'SPANGLE' IN A BOWL OF FLOUR. AND THERE ARE LOTS OF GIRLS WITH BIG BOSOMS. WELL, THERE'S ONE GIRL WITH BIG BOSOMS, AND SHE HATES ME. ACTUALLY, I WANT TO KILL HER.

I'LL JOIN. IT SOUNDS LIKE MY SORT OF THING.

AND SO, IN AN INSTANT, JOHN MADE THE FATEFUL, TRAGIC DECISION TO JOIN THE YOUNG CONSERVATIVES.

JOHN ENJOYED HIS ASSOCIATION WITH THE BRIXTON YOUNG CONSERVATIVES.

NOW THEN, BOYS AND GIRLS. IT'S TIME FOR 'TAKE YOUR PARTNER IN THE DARK'. SO, WHEN I TURN THE LIGHTS OFF, YOU WALK TO THE MIDDLE OF THE ROOM, AND THEN DANCE WITH THE FIRST PERSON YOU TOUCH.

HMM. CUCUMBER SANDWICHES, IF I'M NOT MISTAKEN.

OOH!

TEE-HEE!

GET YOUR HAND OUT OF THERE!

AND NOW IT'S LIGHTS ON AGAIN TIME!

YOU DIRTY BEAST!

MUNCH, MUNCH.

YUK! WHAT'S THIS STUFF ALL DOWN MY FRONT?

HEE, HEE!

AARGH!

THIS WAS A POPULAR ACTIVITY ...

... AND A SOURCE OF MUCH HILARITY.

MUNCH, MUNCH.

RIGHT, BOYS AND GIRLS, TUCK INTO THE SANDWICHES.

URP!

DESPITE THE FUN, THERE WAS A SERIOUS ASPECT TO BEING A YOUNG CONSERVATIVE: IN ORDER TO PREPARE THOSE WHO ASPIRED TO BE POLITICIANS, EVENINGS WERE SET ASIDE FOR MEMBERS TO PRACTISE THEIR SKILLS AT PUBLIC SPEAKING. JOHN MAJOR EXCELLED IN THIS ENDEAVOUR.

YAWN! TIME'S UP, JOHN.

THE ICHNEUMON FLY IS ACTUALLY A SORT OF WASP* - UNLIKE THE CODLING MOTH WHICH IS A ... UM ... MOTH. OH YES. IT HAS AN OVIPOSITOR WHICH IS OF A NOT INCONSIDERABLE LENGTH, AND WHICH IS OF SUFFICIENT STRENGTH TO PENETRATE UNDERPANTS OF UP TO HALF AN INCH THICK. THIS IS WHY YOU SHOULD TUCK YOUR SHIRT INTO YOUR UNDERPANTS. WOMEN HAVE TO MAKE THEIR OWN ARRANGEMENTS IN THIS MATTER. THE CODLING MOTH ...

JOHN NOW DIVIDED HIS TIME BETWEEN MAKING GNOMES DURING THE DAY AND THE YOUNG CONSERVATIVES IN THE EVENINGS. DURING THE 1961 LONDON COUNTY COUNCIL ELECTIONS, HE CAMPAIGNED VIGOROUSLY ON BEHALF OF THE CONSERVATIVE CANDIDATE.

GOOD MORNING. MAY I ASK IF IT IS YOUR INTENTION TO VOTE FOR MR. PINE, HERE? IN MY JUDGEMENT, HE IS, AND IN NO SMALL MEASURE, NOT INCONSIDERABLY BETTER THAN THE LABOURITE CANDIDATE, AND ...

BUGGER OFF!

THE CANDIDATE WAS UNSUCCESSFUL. BUT, FOR JOHN, THE EXPERIENCE OF REJECTION WOULD PROVE VALUABLE IN LATER YEARS.

THE SAME CANDIDATE WAS UNSUCCESSFUL THREE YEARS LATER WHEN, ONCE AGAIN, JOHN CANVASSED ENTHUSIASTICALLY IN HIS SUPPORT.

THANKS A BUNCH FOR ALL YOU'VE DONE FOR MY CAREER, JOHN.

OH, DON'T MENTION IT, LEN. IT'S BEEN A PLEASURE.

BUGGER OFF!

MIEOW!

JOHN WAS ALSO REQUIRED TO RECRUIT NEW MEMBERS INTO THE YOUNG CONSERVATIVE MOVEMENT. ONE WET SATURDAY EVENING HE FOUND HIMSELF OUTSIDE THE LOCAL CHURCH.

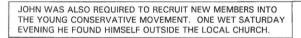

SAINT BRENDA'S
ON THE GREEN

MEETING
TONITE.
ALMOST EVERY-
ONE WELCOME.
BRING YOUR
OWN BOOZE.

HMMM. 'MEETING TONIGHT. EVERYONE WELCOME'. I WILL GAIN ADMISSION TO THIS MEETING, AND, WHEN IT IS PRUDENT TO DO SO, WILL ENDEAVOUR TO GATHER NEW SUPPLIES OF PEOPLE FOR THE CONSERVATIVE PARTY. OH YES.

THE CHURCH DOOR WAS OPENED BY A STRIKINGLY ATTRACTIVE BRUNETTE.

OH, GOD! IT'S HIM! THE GORGEOUS GREY HUNK FROM OPPOSITE MY PLACE!

WELL, HELLO. WOULD YOU LIKE TO COME IN AND JOIN US?

ER ... BUT I WANT YOU TO COME AND JOIN US, SO I WON'T BE ABLE TO JOIN YOU, I'M AFRAID. OH NO.

JOHN RETURNED HOME IN A STATE OF CONSIDERABLE AGITATION.

IN MY JUDGEMENT, SON, YOU ARE IN A STATE OF EXTREME PERTURBATION, AND NOT INCONSIDERABLY SO. OH YES.

I HOPE YOU'RE NOT CONSORTING WITH YOUNG WOMEN AT YOUR YOUNG CONSERVATIVES.

JOHN TRIED HARD TO PUT HIS VOLUPTUOUS NEIGHBOUR OUT OF HIS MIND. TO THIS END HE ACQUIRED A HAMSTER. IN HIS BOOK, MAJOR-MAJOR, TERRY MOVINGLY DESCRIBES THIS ANIMAL AS A WELL-LOVED AND GOOD-NATURED CREATURE THAT NEVER ATTACKED, EVEN WHEN WOKEN FROM ITS SLUMBER BY A DEEP PROD.

COME ON, RISE AND SHINE.

OH, SHIT! NOT ANOTHER DAY TRAIPSING IN THAT BLOODY WHEEL! WHEN I SNUFF IT, I'M COMING BACK AS A GABOON VIPER; THEN NO BUGGER'LL BUGGER WITH ME.

ALAS, THE LITTLE HAMSTER DEVELOPED A SEVERE FORM OF DROPSY, AND BEGAN TO SWELL UP ALARMINGLY.

AUTHOR'S NOTE: THIS ISN'T REALLY VERY EXCITING, BUT LIVENS UP A DULL BIT IN JOHN'S LIFE - NOT THAT ANY PART OF HIS LIFE HAS BEEN, IN ANY WAY, DULL. OH NO.

JOHN - EVER THE ANIMAL LOVER - DID ALL HE COULD TO KEEP THE - BY NOW HUGE - RODENT ALIVE, BUT TO NO AVAIL. ONE DAY IT SIMPLY BLEW ITSELF TO SMITHEREENS.

OH DEAR!

SCREEPYOUIPMIOMEOW...KABLAM!

ACCORDING TO TERRY MAJOR - IN HIS BOOK, MAJOR MAJOR - WHAT WAS LEFT OF THE HAMSTER WAS BURIED WITH FULL MILITARY HONOURS. JUST HOW JOHN MANAGED TO PERSUADE THE POWERS THAT BE AT THE LOCAL ARMY BARRACKS TO TURN OUT AN HONOUR GUARD FOR A RODENT ISN'T AT ALL CLEAR. BUT IT SEEMS LIKELY THAT HIS APTITUDE FOR OBSEQUIOUS CAJOLERY STEMS FROM AROUND THIS TIME.

HONOUR GUARD - FIRE!

WITH THE HAMSTER NO LONGER AVAILABLE AS A MEANS OF DIVERTING HIS THOUGHTS FROM THE ALLURING NEIGHBOUR ACROSS THE ROAD, JOHN TOOK TO RECORDING TOP OF THE POPS ON A REEL-TO-REEL RECORDER. GWEN MAJOR OWNED A BUDGERIGAR, AND THIS MUSICAL BIRD WOULD SING ALONG HAPPILY WITH THE TUNES.

"I WANNA ROBOT MAN ... "

♩ I GOTTA ROBOT MAN ... ♪

♪ I WANNA HOLD YOUR GLANS ... ♪

"I WANNA HOLD YOUR HAND ... "

♪. IN BURTON ROAD, OH YES. ♪

"THERE IS A HOUSE IN ..."

JOHN'S EFFORTS TO SILENCE THIS BIRD WERE UNSUCCESSFUL, AND ALL HIS RECORDINGS ENDED UP WITH AN ADDITIONAL UNWANTED ARTIST ON THEM.

♩ ROBOT MAN. ♪ ROBOT MAN.

WORK AT THE GNOME FACTORY CONTINUED. BUT IT WAS BECOMING OBVIOUS THAT, AFTER YEARS OF MAKING THESE ORNAMENTS, TERRY WAS REACHING THE END OF HIS TETHER.

WHAT DO YOU THINK, JOHN? EH? IT'S A NEW LINE I'VE BEEN DEVELOPING - GNOMES FOR THE SWINGING SIXTIES. WAIT TILL YOU SEE THIS COUPLE UNDER HERE.

I DON'T THINK I WANT TO, TERRY. HAS FATHER SEEN THIS?

AND SO, JOHN NOW MADE GNOMES DURING THE DAY AND STUDIED FOR HIS BANKING EXAMS AT JEAN COLLINS' FLAT DURING THE EVENINGS. IT WAS AN ARRANGEMENT THAT DID NOT MEET WITH HIS MOTHER'S APPROVAL.

AND WHAT TIME DO YOU CALL THIS? I KNOW WHERE YOU'VE BEEN; YOU'VE BEEN WITH THAT COLLINS WOMAN, HAVEN'T YOU? WELL, YOU'VE BROKEN MY HEART. AND YOUR POOR FATHER HARDLY COLD IN HIS GRAVE. I HOPE YOU'RE PLEASED WITH YOURSELF.

BUT MOTHER ...

GWEN WOULD NOT BE MOLLIFIED.

AND TO THINK OF ALL THAT YOUR DEAR FATHER AND I'VE DONE FOR YOU; A GNOME FACTORY ALL OF YOUR OWN! WHAT MORE COULD ANY YOUNG MAN ASK FOR?...

NO, DON'T TELL ME. YOU GO BACK TO YOUR HUSSY...

BUT MOTHER ...

MOTHER? DON'T YOU CALL ME 'MOTHER'. I'M JUST THE POOR OLD WOMAN FROM WHOSE WOMB SPRANG THE MONSTER I SEE BEFORE ME - MAY THE GOOD LORD HAVE MERCY ON MY SOUL.

BUT MOTHER, IT'S TEA TIME.

WHA...? SO IT IS. SHEPHERD'S PIE ALL RIGHT?

THE EVENINGS OF STUDY AT MRS. COLLINS' FLAT WERE BECOMING NO LESS TRYING FOR JOHN. AND FOR MRS. COLLINS, FOR THAT MATTER.

HONEYBUN? JEAN'S GETTING AWFULLY LONESOME PLAYING WITH HER SUEDE DOGGY-WOGGY.

BUT I BOUGHT IT SO YOU'D HAVE SOMETHING TO TALK TO, JEAN.

I KNOW YOU DID, HONEYBUNNY. BUT YOU KNOW WHAT THEY SAY; ALL WORK AND NO PLAY MAKES JACK A DULL BOY.

AH, BUT MY NAME IS NOT JACK. IT IS, IN FACT, JOHN.

JOHN'S SKILL AS A TOILSOME DEBATER DATES FROM AROUND THIS TIME.

JEAN WAS FALLING IN LOVE. AND, ALTHOUGH SHE WAS CONSIDERABLY OLDER THAN JOHN, AND HAD BEEN MARRIED AND DIVORCED SOME YEARS PREVIOUSLY, SHE FOUND IT DIFFICULT TO DECLARE HER FEELINGS FOR SOMEONE WHO SEEMED SO DETERMINEDLY CLUELESS.

OOH. I JUST LOVE THIS RECORD, DON'T YOU?

IT'S QUITE NICE. BUT I LIKE THIS NEW RECORD: "MY PULLOVER" BY JESS CONRAD, WHICH, IN MY JUDGEMENT, SHOULD BE A NUMBER ONE HIT.

♪ I WANT TO BE LOVED BY YOU, ♫ JUST YOU AND NOBODY ELSE BUT YOU ...

♪ "MY PULLOVER, MY PULLOVER. I'M VERY FOND OF MY PULLOVER". I'LL GET IT FOR YOU, IF YOU LIKE.

JEAN EMPLOYED A VARIETY OF DEVIOUS RUSES TO DISTRACT JOHN FROM HIS STUDIES ...

" TONIGHT, TONIGHT WON'T BE JUST ANY NIGHT. BUT WILL HE LOVE ME TOMORROW ..." WHAT YOU DON'T KNOW, HONEYBUNNY, IS THAT I ONLY PUT A SHILLING IN THE METER, AND THAT THE LIGHTS ARE GOING OUT ANY MINUTE NOW! THEN ...

ON THE OTHER SIDE OF THE ROAD, GWEN WAS KEEPING A CONSTANT VIGIL.

I CAN SEE YOU. I CAN SEE YOU. OH YES.

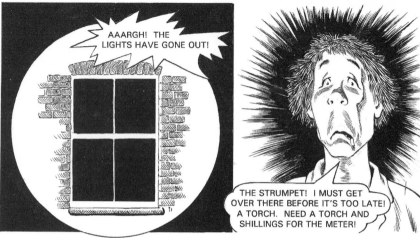

DESPITE HIS MOTHER'S OBJECTIONS, JOHN CONTINUED TO SPEND LONG EVENINGS WITH JEAN. WHILE THE TWO WOMEN STILL COMPETED FOR JOHN'S ATTENTION, A SORT OF TRUCE DEVELOPED BETWEEN THEM. BEFORE LONG THEY BECAME A NEARLY INSEPARABLE THREESOME, SHARING MANY OF THE LONG SUMMER DAYS TOGETHER.
ALTHOUGH HER NAME WAS JEAN, JOHN BEGAN TO CALL HER MARY - JUST WHY IS YET ANOTHER EXAMPLE OF THE RIDDLE THAT IS THE MYSTERY WRAPPED IN THE ENIGMA THAT IS JOHN MAJOR. JEAN, ON THE OTHER HAND, BEGAN TO REFER TO JOHN AS 'RAVE', THOUGH TO THIS DAY SHE CANNOT THINK WHY.

THERE'S A GOOD CRICKET MATCH ON IN THE COUNTRY.

I'D LIKE THAT, RAVE.

I HATES CRICKET.

AS OFTEN AS NOT THE THREE OF THEM WOULD END UP WATCHING FOOTBALL.

I HATES FOOTBALL.

JEAN LEARNED A GREAT DEAL FROM JOHN. LESSONS SHE WOULD NEVER FORGET.

I WANTS A PICKLED EGG.

YOU MUST PUT THE VINEGAR ON FIRST, OTHERWISE IT WASHES ALL THE SALT AWAY. WHEREAS, IF YOU PUT THE SALT ON AFTER THE VINEGAR, THE SALT REMAINS ... ER ... VISIBLE TO THE EYE.

OH, RAVE. YOU'RE SO CLEVER.

SOMETIMES THEY'D HIRE A BOAT FROM A MR. HERMANN GOERING AND MEANDER UP THE RIVER AND INTO THE COUNTRYSIDE. JEAN WAS IMPRESSED BY JOHN'S SKILL AT THE HELM. ✳

HOVE-HEE! SPLICE THE GIBLETS! HEAVE-TO A YANFLANKS! HOISE THE SAVALOY!

OH, RAVE. THIS IS JUST SO FAB'! JUST YOU AND ME, THE SUEDE DOG AND YOUR OLD MUM.

✳ SEE THE LINDA LEE-POTTER INTERVIEW. MAIL ON SUNDAY AND DAILY MAIL, FEB' 12 AND 13 1995.

DESPITE THESE TRIBULATIONS, JOHN CONTINUED WITH HIS STUDIES AND PASSED PART I OF THE INSTITUTE OF BANKERS EXAMS SOMETIME IN 1966. EQUIPPED WITH HIS NEWLY ACQUIRED QUALIFICATIONS, HE QUICKLY GAINED EMPLOYMENT WITH 'THE AMALGAMATED STRANGLEHOLD BANK', ONE OF THE BIGGEST OF INTERNATIONAL USURERS.

RIGHT, MAJOR. YOUR JOB IS TO CHANGE THE BIROS, AND ENSURE THEY'RE SECURELY CHAINED TO THE COUNTER ON THE LEFT-HANDED SIDE OF THE TELLERS' WINDOWS. MOST OF OUR CUSTOMERS ARE RIGHT-HANDED, AND WE DON'T WANT TO MAKE THEIR WRETCHED LITTLE LIVES EASIER, DO WE?

GOOD, GOOD. WELL, HERE WE ARE: THE EGG PLANT. NOW THIS PLANT HAS BEEN WITH US SINCE THE MIDDLE OF LAST WEEK, SO YOU CAN SEE IT'S SOMETHING OF AN OLD FRIEND. APART FROM REGULAR WATERING, IT LIKES TO HAVE ITS LEAVES SPONGED WITH MILK EVERY OTHER WEEK. MANAGE THAT, CAN YOU, MAJOR?

OH YES.

PROMOTION CAME QUICKLY FOR THE ENTHUSIASTIC JOHN MAJOR.

THE POWERS THAT BE ARE PLEASED WITH THE WAY YOU'VE HANDLED THE BIROS, MAJOR. WORD REACHES ME YOU'RE TO BE INVESTED WITH A FURTHER DUTY. FOLLOW ME, BOY.

OH, GOODY. I'VE ENJOYED WORKING WITH BIROS. BUT FEEL I'M READY FOR A MORE TAXING TASK.

AND PROMOTION FOLLOWED PROMOTION, UNTIL ONE DAY ...

AH, MAJOR. POWERS THAT BE WOULD LIKE YOU TO VOLUNTEER TO HELP OUT IN ONE OF OUR WEST AFRICAN BRANCHES. JOHNNY DARKIE'S ON THE RAMPAGE AND MOST OF OUR CHAPS OUT THERE HAVE BUGGERED OFF INTO THE BUSH, AND WE NEED A VOLUNTEER - NAY, A 'TROUBLE-SHOOTER' - TO GET OUT AND SHAG SOME BLOODY SENSE INTO OUR TINTED BRETHREN, O.K? GOOD. GET PETTY CASH TO BUNG YOU A HUNDRED, AND GO OFF AND GET SOME KIT: THE FUZZY-WUZZIES RESPECT A CHAP IN A PITH-HELMET.

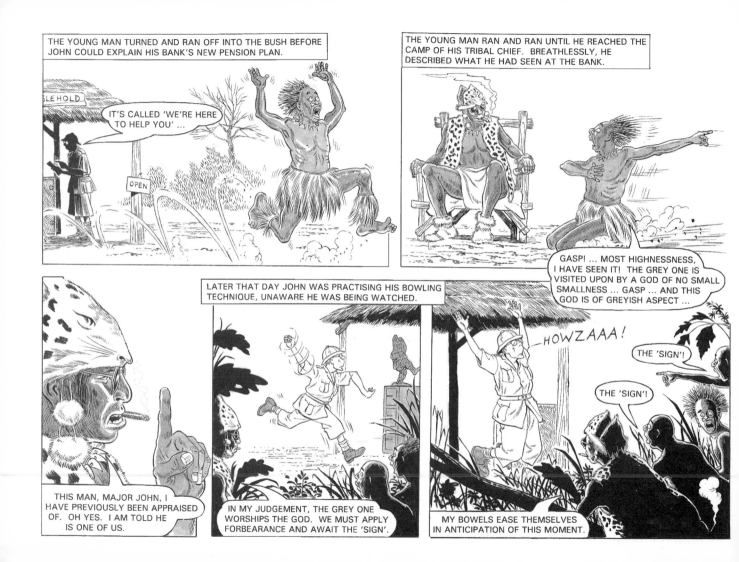

INEXPLICABLY, RICHARD LEAPT FROM THE CAR BEFORE IT CRASHED.

WHEN THE CAR LEFT THE ROAD IT WAS PROBABLY DOING 220 MILES PER HOUR.

THE CAR PLUNGED INTO A RAVINE ...

STORKS ARE QUITE DIFFICULT TO MAKE DUE TO THE FACT THAT THEY HAVE LONG SPINDLY LEGS ...

... SOMERSAULTING SEVERAL TIMES ...

... BEFORE SMASHING INTO TWENTY-TON BOULDERS AT THE BOTTOM AND EXPLODING IN A FIREBALL THAT COULD BE SEEN FOR MILES.

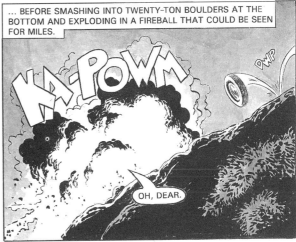

AS LUCK WOULD HAVE IT, SEVERAL HAUSA TRIBESMEN WERE CAMPED NEARBY ATTENDING THE MONTHLY MEETING OF THE BUKARU AND JOS DISTRICT ELVIS PRESLEY FAN CLUB.

GREAT LIGHT AND A NOT INCONSIDERABLE THUNDERING TO THE EAST!

YOU CALL ME 'HOUND DOG'? YOU BRING DISHONOUR TO MY MOTHER.

NO. YOUR FOOLISHNESS REACHES TO THE HEAVENS. HOUND DOG IS THE WORDS OF 'THE KING' ON THIS BLACK CIRCLE.

THE TRIBESMEN RACED TO THE SOURCE OF THE LIGHT.

I OFFER YOU MY WIFE. YOU GIVE ME ELVIS JACKET.

YOUR OFFER IS OF NO USE TO ME. I AM OBLIGED TO PASS MY WATERS OVER IT.

SOON THEY ARRIVED AT THE SCENE OF THE ACCIDENT.

IN MY JUDGEMENT, NO MORTAL BEING CAN WALK FROM THIS DIABOLICAL INFERNO.

BUT WAIT! OVER THERE! IT IS THE GREY ONE. AND HE LIVES!

THE GODS HAVE BEEN MERCIFUL. GREATNESS IS TO BE THRUST UPON HIM.

JOHN HAD HAD A MIRACULOUS ESCAPE, ALTHOUGH HE HAD BROKEN HIS LEG IN SEVERAL PLACES. THE TRIBESMEN QUICKLY FASHIONED A MAKESHIFT STRETCHER AND RAN THROUGH THE NIGHT WITH HIM TO THE AIRFIELD AT JOS.

LITTLE RICHARD VERSION OF 'TUTTI FRUTTI' NOT AS GOOD AS ELVIS.

AN ABUNDANCE OF GUANO OCCUPIES YOUR WHOLE BEING, ENBAGI.

THEY REACHED THE LITTLE AIRFIELD JUST AS AN AIRCRAFT WAS BEGINNING TO TAXI DOWN THE RUNWAY.

GREAT SILVER BIRD IS ABOUT TO FLY! WE MUST DEPOSIT THE GREY ONE WITHIN ITS BELLY SO THAT HE MAY BE BORNE TO GODS THAT HEAL!

THE FOUR MONTHS JOHN SPENT IN AFRICA WOULD MORE THAN PREPARE HIM FOR THE THREE MONTHS HE WOULD LATER SPEND AS FOREIGN SECRETARY.

THUNK

AFTER A LONG AND PAINFUL JOURNEY OUT OF AFRICA, JOHN ARRIVED IN LONDON. HE WAS RUSHED FROM THE AIRPORT TO THE MAYHEM HOSPITAL IN CROYDON.

THE STAFF AT THE HOSPITAL WENT TO WORK ON JOHN'S SHATTERED LEG AND SOON HAD IT SAFELY ENCASED IN PLASTER. WITHIN A FEW DAYS, JOHN RECEIVED HIS FIRST VISITORS.

ELVIS MIGHT'VE PUT A BIT OF WEIGHT ON, BUT HE'S STILL 'THE KING'.

BOLLOCKS! CLIFF'S 'THE KING' NOW MATE.

I LIKE JESS CONRAD.

JESS CONRAD! HE'S RUBBISH, HE IS. I WOULDN'T PISS ON HIM IF HE WAS BURNING TO DEATH IN THE STREET, MATE. THAT'S WHAT I THINK ABOUT JESS CONRAD.

HONEY-BUNNY!

STAND ASIDE! LET ME GET TO MY LITTLE WOUNDED SOLDIER!

JOHN FOUND THE MINISTRATIONS OF THESE TWO STRONG-WILLED WOMEN HARD TO COPE WITH.

I'VE TALKED AT THE DOCTORS AND TOLD THEM I'LL LAY DOWN MY LIFE FOR YOU, IF NECESSARY. THEY TOLD ME THAT WOULD BE A BIT DRASTIC AS YOU'VE ONLY BROKEN YOUR LEG - ONLY BROKEN YOUR LEG! I MEAN, IF YOU WERE LIKE A BIG HAIRY SPIDER WITH LOTS OF LEGS, IT MIGHT NOT MATTER. BUT YOU'VE ONLY GOT TWO! ... SOB! AND ONE OF THOSE IS SMASHED INTO TINY LITTLE PIECES!

DOES RAVE'S POOR LITTLE LEG ITCH? WOULD HE LIKE ME TO SCRATCH IT FOR HIM?

THAT'S THE WRONG LEG, MARY.

AND TERRY DROPPED BY TO SEE HIS STRICKEN BROTHER.

I'VE HAD ENOUGH OF GNOMES, TO TELL YOU THE TRUTH, JOHN. I'M GOING INTO CHRISTMAS TREES. MET A BLOKE WHO RECKONS CHRISTMAS TREES'LL BE BIG BY THE END OF THE YEAR.

AS IT TURNED OUT, TERRY'S VISITS WOULD PROVE CRUCIAL TO JOHN'S RECOVERY.

... ANYWAY, THIS BLOKE I KNOW SAYS JULY'S ALWAYS A BIT SLOWISH FOR CHRISTMAS TREES, SO I'M NOT TOO BOTHERED. TELL YOU WHAT, THOUGH, JOHN; IF I WERE YOU I'D BE MORE THAN A BIT BOTHERED ABOUT THE WAY THAT LEG OF YOURS IS SETTING.

TERRY WAS RIGHT TO BE CONCERNED: THE DOCTORS HAD SET JOHN'S LEG BADLY.

WELL, MAJOR. IT WOULD SEEM THAT YOUR TIBIA AND FIBULA ARE MISALIGNED BY 180 DEGREES. IN OTHER WORDS, YOUR LEFT FOOT'S FACING THE WRONG WAY. THIS IS A COMMON OCCURRENCE WITH THIS SORT OF INJURY. ANYWAY, WE HAVE WHAT WE MEDICS LIKE TO CALL 'OPTIONS' TO CONSIDER HERE: WE CAN BREAK AND RESET YOUR RIGHT LEG SO THAT IT ASSUMES THE SAME ALIGNMENT AS YOUR LEFT LEG. THE BEAUTY OF THIS OPTION IS THAT IT MAKES LEANING BACKWARDS MUCH EASIER. LEANING FORWARDS, HOWEVER, BECOMES A BIT OF A PROBLEM.

JOHN BROODED ON THE OPTIONS HE'D BEEN GIVEN, FINALLY DECIDING IT WOULD BE BEST IF BOTH FEET FACED FORWARDS IN ORDER TO AVOID THE POSSIBILITY OF FALLING FLAT ON HIS FACE AT A FUTURE DATE.

HIS LEG RESET, JOHN BEGAN A LONG CONVALESCENCE. APART FROM EATING HUGE QUANTITIES OF GRAPES AND BANANAS, HE BEGAN TO READ. IT WAS DURING THIS TIME HE BECAME ACQUAINTED WITH A TROLLOP.

AUTHOR'S NOTE: THE AUTHOR WISHES TO APOLOGISE TO READERS WHO, HAVING READ THE BLURB ON THE BACK OF THIS BOOK, MIGHT'VE EXPECTED SOMETHING A LITTLE MORE EXCITING THAN THIS.

THE REGULARITY OF JOHN'S BOWEL MOVEMENTS HAD LONG BEEN OF CONCERN TO GWEN. AND THEY WERE BEGINNING NOW TO BECOME A MATTER OF SOME DISTRESS TO JOHN. WITH HIS LEG STILL IN PLASTER, JOHN FOUND IT DIFFICULT TO GET UPSTAIRS TO THE LAVATORY. THERE WAS AN OUTSIDE LOO IN THE GARDEN ...,

ALLOW ME.

... BUT, ALTHOUGH IT WAS EASIER TO GET TO, THE SMALL PROPORTIONS OF THIS BUILDING COUPLED WITH HIS PLASTERED LEG CONSPIRED TO CONFOUND JOHN'S INCREASINGLY EARNEST DESIRE FOR PRIVACY.

HEH HEH HOO

OH DAMN AND BOTHERATION!

IT HAS BEEN SUGGESTED THAT THIS IRREGULAR AND INSUFFICIENT MOVEMENT OF THE BOWELS - OR 'CONSTIPATION' AS THE CONDITION IS MORE COMMONLY REFERRED TO - AND THE ANXIETIES IT MUST HAVE PRODUCED IN THE YOUNG JOHN MAJOR, MIGHT ACCOUNT FOR HIS RATHER WOODEN DELIVERY AT THE DISPATCH BOX IN THE HOUSE OF COMMONS.

I REFER THE HONOURABLE ANSWER TO THE GENTLEMENS.

EVENTUALLY, JOHN COULD NO LONGER STOMACH HIS MOTHER'S ATTENTIONS, AND HE MOVED TO A TINY BEDSIT AT 9 TEMPLAR STREET, BRIXTON.

YOU'RE AN UNGRATEFUL AND HORRIBLE BASTARD! WELL, DON'T COME CRAWLING BACK HERE IF YOU GET STUNG TO DEATH BY A SWARM OF KILLER BEES BECAUSE I'LL PROBABLY HAVE DIED OF ANOTHER BROKEN HEART!

CAN I HAVE JOHN'S TEA, MUM?

HIS BRUSH WITH DEATH HAD CONVINCED JOHN THAT BANKING WASN'T FOR HIM. INSTEAD HE PLUNGED INTO LOCAL POLITICS. A FRIEND ADVISED HIM TO STAND FOR WHAT WAS THOUGHT TO BE A SAFE LABOUR SEAT IN THE LAMBETH BOROUGH COUNCIL ELECTIONS IN MAY 1968.

YOU DON'T STAND A CHANCE OF WINNING THE FERNHURST WARD SEAT, JOHN. SO, WHY DON'T YOU TRY FOR IT?

JOHN'S FRIEND COULDN'T HAVE BEEN MORE MISTAKEN: IT SO HAPPENED AN ECCENTRIC TORY MP HAD RECENTLY MADE A WIDELY REPORTED PREDICTION THAT, UNLESS IMMIGRATION WAS HALTED, THE STREETS OF GREAT BRITAIN WOULD BE TURNED INTO RIVERS OF BLOOD, AND THAT, CONSEQUENTLY, PEOPLE WOULD BE OBLIGED TO GO TO WORK IN SMALL BOATS. MANY PREVIOUSLY SANE LABOUR VOTERS BECAME ALARMED AT THIS PROSPECT AND VOTED FOR TORY CANDIDATES, SOME OF WHOM CANVASSED UNDER THE SLOGANS "YES TO STREETS - NO TO BLOODY CANALS", AND "WE BACK A COMPLETE LOONY". TO HIS CREDIT, JOHN HAD NOTHING TO DO WITH THIS SORT OF CAMPAIGNING. NEVERTHELESS, HE BENEFITED FROM IT, WINNING THE FERNHURST WARD FOR THE TORIES HAND-SOMELY. HIS POLITICAL CAREER HAD BEGUN.

HOORAY! LAMBETH BELONGS TO US!

HURRAH!

AFTER THE RESULTS OF THE COUNCIL ELECTIONS HAD BEEN ANNOUNCED, JOHN MADE HIS WAY HOME WITH SOME FELLOW REVELLERS. THEIR HIGH SPIRITS NEARLY LANDED JOHN IN SERIOUS TROUBLE.

'ERE WE GO, 'ERE WE GO.

C'MON, JOHN, LET'S WAKE THE WHOLE BLOODY STREET UP AND TELL 'EM WE'RE IN POWER NOW.

WE ARE THE CHAMPIONS!

IN HIS EUPHORIA AT HAVING WON A COUNCIL SEAT, JOHN ALLOWED HIMSELF TO BE HOISTED UP A LAMP POST IN ORDER TO THROW STONES AT THE BEDROOM WINDOW OF AN ELDERLY WOMAN.

NEENAW NEENAW

BLOODY HELL, ROZZERS! LET'S SCARPER, CHAPS!

C'MON YOU OLD BAG, WAKEY WAKEY!

ALMOST IMMEDIATELY, JOHN WAS APPOINTED DEPUTY CHAIRMAN OF THE HOUSING COMMITTEE ON LAMBETH COUNCIL. THIS WAS AN IMPORTANT APPOINTMENT AS IN SOME OF THE MORE RUN-DOWN PARTS OF THE BOROUGH AS MANY AS 200,000 PEOPLE LIVED IN ONE HOUSE. IN OTHER AREAS, WHOLE STREETS WERE COLLAPSING. JOHN WAS FASCINATED BY HOUSES AND ARGUED PASSIONATELY ON THE SUBJECT IN THE COUNCIL CHAMBERS.

IN MY JUDGEMENT, PEOPLE NEED HOUSES. WITHOUT HOUSES THEY ARE HOUSELESS. WE NEED, THEREFORE, TO BUILD HOUSES SO THAT THOSE THAT ARE HOUSELESS BECOME HOUSED. OH YES.

THE IRREFUTABLE LOGIC OF HIS ARGUMENT LED DIRECTLY TO THE DEMOLITION OF WHOLE STREETS AND THE ERECTION OF VAST SKY-SCRAPERS. TO THE PLANNERS THIS WAS THE ANSWER TO ALL HOUSING PROBLEMS. THOSE WHO LIVED AT THE TOP OF THESE CONSTRUCTIONS WERE LESS SURE.

YOUR TURN TO PUT THE BLOODY DOG OUT, DUCKS.

NO IT BLOODY ISN'T!

IT BLOODY IS!

DURING ONE OF HIS MANY INTERVIEWS WITH PENNY JUNOR, JOHN CONCEDES:

ONCE WE HAD BUILT ONE SKY-SCRAPER, THEN WE NEEDED TO BUILD ANOTHER ONE. SOON WE COULDN'T HELP OURSELVES; WE'D TEAR DOWN WHOLE STREETS IN ORDER TO BUILD THEM; THEY SEEMED LIKE A GOOD IDEA AT THE TIME. BUT WE WERE WRONG. IT WAS TERRIBLE ... SOB .

SO YOU BECAME A SERIAL SKY-SCRAPER BUILDER, DID YOU, JOHN?

OH YES.

ALTHOUGH JOHN RELISHED HIS TIME AS VICE CHAIRMAN OF THE HOUSING COMMITTEE, HE WAS BEGINNING TO DEVELOP PARLIAMENTARY AMBITIONS. TO THIS END HE CAMPAIGNED ENTHUSIASTICALLY IN SUPPORT OF THE LOCAL MP'S SUCCESSFUL ATTEMPT TO GET FOX HUNTING BANNED IN BRIXTON - DOUBTLESS MUCH TO THE FURY OF THE LOCAL LANDED GENTRY.

WE MUST PURGE AND SPONGE FROM OUR STREETS THE SIGHT OF MEN ON HORSEBACK PURSUING FOXES - WHICH YOU CAN'T EAT ANYWAY, BECAUSE THEY PROBABLY TASTE NASTY - WELL, YOU COULD IF THERE WAS A SHORTAGE OF OTHER THINGS TO EAT LIKE CHICKENS AND SAUSAGES WHICH THERE ISN'T ... ER ...

AYE?

WHAT'S 'E BLEEDING ON ABOUT?

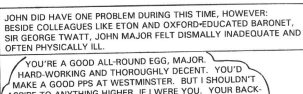

AND WHILE NORMA IS PRACTICAL, PENNY JUNOR DESCRIBES JOHN AS BEING 'HOPELESS'.

AH, NORMA. I'VE JUST RETURNED FROM THE COUNCIL CHAMBERS TO FIND THAT THE HOUSE IS IN TOTAL DARKNESS.

NOW LISTEN, JOHN. GO TO THE DOOR YOU'VE JUST ENTERED. NOW, USING YOUR HAND, FEEL FOR A ROUND PLASTIC THING ON THE WALL NEAR THE DOOR FRAME AND ABOUT FOUR AND A HALF FEET FROM THE FLOOR. IN THE MIDDLE OF THIS ROUND THING YOU'LL FIND A LITTLE BUTTON POINTING TO THE CEILING. PUSH THIS BUTTON DOWNWARDS SO THAT IT POINTS TO THE FLOOR. THIS ACTION SHOULD SOLVE YOUR PROBLEM.

WHAT WOULD I DO WITHOUT YOU, NORMA?

GOD KNOWS. BUT I'M BEGINNING TO WONDER WHAT I MIGHT DO WITHOUT YOU, JOHN.

IN NO SMALL MEASURE, THAT'S THE NICEST THING ANYONE HAS EVER SAID TO ME IN MY ENTIRE LIFE, TO DATE.

DURING SEPTEMBER OF THAT YEAR GWEN DIED. THE LITTLE TOBACCONIST SHE HAD FREQUENTED FOR SO MANY YEARS CLOSED ITS DOOR AS A TOUCHING MARK OF RESPECT.

WE'RE FINISHED! THE OLD GIRL'S FALLEN OFF HER PERCH! SHE SPENT A FORTUNE IN HERE!

OPEN UP, OPEN UP! I NEED MY CIGARETTES AND A KIT-KAT FOR MY DOG 'CHUNK'.

M. THURSTON: TOBACCONIST

CAT?

DESPITE GWEN'S DEATH, JOHN AND NORMA DECIDED TO GET MARRIED TWO WEEKS LATER. BY ALL ACCOUNTS, IT WAS AN EXTRAORDINARY AFFAIR; JOHN'S LEG HAS NEVER FULLY RECOVERED FROM THE ACCIDENT IN NIGERIA, AND IN TIMES OF STRESS IT LETS HIM DOWN. ON THE DAY OF HIS WEDDING IT GAVE WAY AND HE HAD TO BE CARRIED UP THE AISLE.

DO YOU TAKE THIS WOMAN ...

OH YES. ALTHOUGH SHE IS SOMETHING OF A 'SPEC BUY' IN MY JUDGEMENT.

SEE P63. 'THE MAJOR ENIGMA'.

AFTER A BRIEF HONEYMOON, JOHN RETURNED TO THE HURLY-BURLY OF LAMBETH POLITICS. ALTHOUGH THE TORY GROUP HAD SWEPT THE BOARD IN 1968 COUNCIL ELECTIONS, THE VOTERS IN THE BOROUGH HAD BEEN OVERCOME BY SOME SORT OF COLLECTIVE AND PERVERSE URGE TO VOTE AGAINST THEIR USUAL INSTINCT. THE NATION SUCCUMBED TO THE SAME ABERRANT COMPULSION DURING THE 1992 GENERAL ELECTION. DURING THE COUNCIL ELECTIONS OF 1971 THE VOTERS OF LAMBETH REVERTED TO TYPE AND BOOTED THE TORIES OUT OF OFFICE. ACCORDING TO SOME NATIONAL NEWSPAPERS, THE LAMBETH COUNCIL CHAMBERS HAVE SINCE BECOME THE PRESERVE OF LUNATICS AND SEXUAL DEVIANTS. IT SEEMS THE GOOD PEOPLE OF LAMBETH PREFER WHAT HAS BECOME KNOWN AS 'LOONY LEFT COUNCILLORS' TO, WELL, TORY COUNCILLORS LIKE JOHN.

VOTE LABOUR

UNRUFFLED BY THIS REJECTION, JOHN DECIDED IT WAS TIME TO TRY HIS HAND AT NATIONAL POLITICS. NORMA WAS VERY UPSET.

MY GENERAL PREDISPOSITION REMAINS REMARKABLY UNPERTURBED BY THIS SET-BACK WHICH IS NOT A SET-BACK AT ALL, OH NO. RATHER IT IS A STEPPING STONE.

HONK

I WISH YOU'D GIVE ALL THIS NONSENSE UP AND GO BACK TO YOUR BANKING THING, JOHN.

BUT JOHN HAD HAD ENOUGH OF BANKING: HE FOUND IT BORING; AND, IN NO SMALL MEASURE, DANGEROUS. INSTEAD HE APPLIED HIMSELF TO THE TASK OF GETTING SELECTED AS A PARLIAMENTARY CANDIDATE. ONCE AGAIN, HIS FRIEND AT THE LOCAL CONSERVATIVE PARTY ASSOCIATION URGED HIM TO APPLY FOR A SEAT HE HAD NO CHANCE OF WINNING, ST. PANCRAS. AFTER SEVERAL INTERVIEWS WITH JOHN, THE ST. PANCRAS CPA DECIDED TO GIVE HIM A CHANCE. CONSERVATIVE CENTRAL OFFICE DID NOT APPROVE OF THEIR CHOICE.

WE'VE BEEN GOING THROUGH YOUR CANDIDATE'S C.V., TONY. GNOME MAKING IN WORCESTER PARK? BROKEN LEG IN BONGO BONGO LAND? LAMBETH NOW TWINNED WITH MOSCOW? UP HERE WE'RE NONE TOO IMPRESSED, I HAVE TO TELL YOU.

BUGGER THE CANDIDATE, GILES. HE'S GOT THIS AGENT CALLED SUE SUMMERS. SHE'S NEW TO THE GAME. NO EXPERIENCE OF HANDLING CANDIDATES, BUT SHE'S GOT FABULOUS TITS. ANYWAY, I THOUGHT AS WE DON'T STAND AN EARTHLY OF WINNING THE BLOODY SEAT I'D CHEER MYSELF UP GIVING HIS AGENT THE ONCE OVER.

AS PREDICTED, JOHN LOST THE ST. PANCRAS SEAT COMFORTABLY. EIGHT MONTHS LATER HE WAS SELECTED TO FIGHT THE SEAT AGAIN. SUE SUMMERS URGED JOHN TO ALTER HIS IMAGE.

LOOK JOHN, YOU'RE A NICE ENOUGH BLOKE AND YOU'VE JUST MISSED BEING QUITE ATTRACTIVE. YOU LOOK LIKE A BLOODY BANKER: ALL GREY AND YUKKY. YOU NEED TO LOOSEN UP. BE A BIT GROOVY.

YOU MEAN LIKE MY BROTHER TERRY. I'LL GIVE IT SOME THOUGHT.

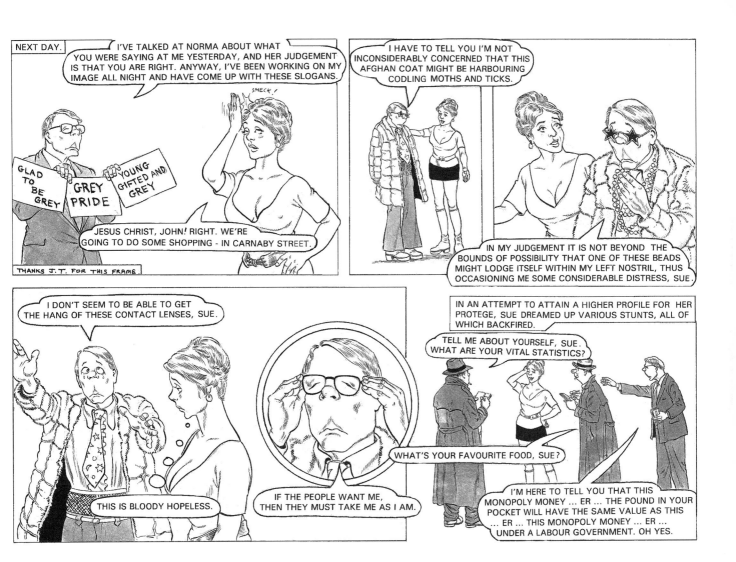

FOR A SECOND TIME, JOHN LOST THE ST. PANCRAS SEAT WITH A THUMPING MINORITY. HE WAS DEEPLY HURT BY THE LABOUR JIBE THAT HIS ATTEMPT TO WIN THE SEAT WAS 'NOT A MAJOR SUCCESS'. HIS LOCAL CONSERVATIVE ASSOCIATION CONTINUED TO DIRECT HIM TO TRY TO GET SELECTED FOR SEATS HE HAD NO HOPE OF WINNING, BUT THE PENNY NEVER DROPPED.

FOR TWO YEARS JOHN TRAIPSED AROUND THE COUNTRY IN AN INCREASINGLY FORLORN ATTEMPT TO GET SELECTED AS A PARLIAMENTARY CANDIDATE. THROUGHOUT HE KEPT IN REGULAR CONTACT WITH HIS LOCAL PARTY OFFICIALS. THEN ONE DAY ...

HELLO. IT'S JOHN HERE ...

JOHN? JOHN WHO?

HUNTINGDON

MAJOR. I'VE FOUND MYSELF IN A PLACE CALLED HUNTINGDON AND WONDERED IF THERE'S A SEAT UP HERE I OUGHT TO TRY FOR.

IT'S THAT BLOODY MAJOR BUGGER AGAIN. HE'S IN HUNTINGDON. WANTS TO KNOW IF THERE'S A SEAT GOING.

DOESN'T GIVE UP, DOES HE? WELL, IT JUST HAPPENS DAVID RENTOKILL'S STANDING DOWN IN HUNTINGDON AT THE NEXT ELECTION. CONSTITUENCY'S PROBABLY STUFFED WITH COLONEL BLIMPS AND BLUE-RINSED OLD BAGS, SO MAJOR WON'T STAND A CHANCE WITH HIS BRIXTON BACKGROUND. TELL HIM TO GO FOR IT.

IT JUST SO HAPPENED THAT HUNTINGDON HAD BECOME HOME FOR HUNDREDS OF THOUSANDS OF REFUGEES FROM BRIXTON AND ST. PANCRAS. THE CONSERVATIVE ASSOCIATION THERE WERE ANXIOUS TO FIND A CANDIDATE WHO COULD RELATE TO THIS HORRIBLE LONDON OVERSPILL. AT LONG LAST, JOHN'S SEARCH FOR A SEAT WAS COMING TO AN END.

I DON'T LIKE IT EITHER, M'DEAR. BUT WE HAVE TO FACE THE FACT THAT OUR COMMUNITY'S CHANGED AND WE NEED A CANDIDATE WHO CAN IDENTIFY WITH THIS SHOWER. THIS BLIGHTER MAJOR SEEMS THE OBVIOUS, IF REGRETTABLE, CHOICE. DAMMIT HE'S ONE OF THEM!

I KNOW, BRIGADIER. I KNOW. BUT HAVE YOU HEARD HIM SPEAK? DEAR LORD, HE SOUNDS LIKE A LAWN MOWER STUCK IN LONG GRASS.

THERE WERE OTHER APPLICANTS , HOWEVER. EVENTUALLY A SHORTLIST OF THREE POTENTIAL CANDIDATES WAS DRAWN UP. EACH WAS TO TO BE INVITED TO SPEAK BEFORE THE SELECTION COMMITTEE FOR SEVERAL MINUTES. THE FIRST TO SPEAK WAS JACK BINGE-MONSTER, AN ECCENTRIC AND 'COLOURFUL' TORY OF THE HUNTIN' SHOOTIN' FISHIN' SCHOOL OF TORY MPs. APPARENTLY HE DID NOT PERFORM WELL.

... ER ... PISH TASH! THASH WHAT I SHAY ... HARUMPH! BLOODY COUNTRY GONE TO THE DOGSH. WELL, THEY'RE WELCOME TO IT, I SHAY. DOGSH A MANSH BESHT FRIEND, DON'T YOU KNOW? WELL, HE ISH. AND DON'T YOU BLOODY FORGET IT. ANYWAY ...

ANOTHER HOPEFUL WAS A MARQUESS. ALTHOUGH HE WAS MUCH FAVOURED BY TRADITIONALIST TORIES ON THE COMMITTEE, HIS PARLIAMENTARY AMBITIONS WERE BLIGHTED IN THE EYES OF SOME FOR BEING MARRIED TO KAISER WILHELM 11's DAUGHTER. OLD ENMITIES DIE HARD IN HUNTINGDONSHIRE. ANYWAY, HIS SPEECH WAS PRETTY HOPELESS.

'JA'? DID HE SAY 'JA?' ISN'T THAT SOME SORT OF JERRY WORD, COLONEL?

I SAY! AWFULLY GOOD TO BE HERE, WHAT. ER … REALLY, REALLY JOLLY SUPER. SUPER DOOPER WHOOPER, ACTUALLY. YAH!

THEN IT WAS JOHN'S TURN. BY ALL ACCOUNTS HE MADE THE SPEECH OF HIS LIFE: JOHN WAS BAFFLING IN HIS CANDOUR; ENTHRALLING IN HIS TEDIOUSNESS; CORUSCATING IN HIS LIFELESSNESS.

… AND SHOULD WE FAIL TO REMEMBER, LET US NOT FORGET THERE'S ALWAYS A CHOICE AS TO WHETHER ONE DOES IT LAST WEEK, THIS WEEK, OR NEXT WEEK . SO IT MUST BE THE TASK OF ALL CONSERVATIVES TO DRIVE THIS MESSAGE HOME. AGAIN AND AGAIN AND AGAIN.

… AND LET ME TELL YOU THIS; IT'S A LONG WAY FROM THE BACK STREETS OF BRIXTON TO THE GREEN FIELDS OF HUNTINGDON - SIXTY MILES, IN FACT. AND IT'S EVEN FURTHER IF YOU GO VIA OSWESTRY.

THE SELECTION COMMITTEE WERE CONVINCED JOHN WAS THEIR MAN.

WELL, I DON'T KNOW ABOUT YOU, M'DEAR, BUT I DIDN'T UNDERSTAND A WORD OF THAT. I RATHER IMAGINE HE MUST BE TALKING IN SOME SORT OF DIALECT PECULIAR TO LONDON. SO I SUPPOSE WE'D BETTER LET HIM BE OUR CANDIDATE, GOD HELP US.

HAVING SWEPT THE OPPOSITION ASIDE WITH THE POWER OF HIS ORATORY, JOHN WAS DULY ELECTED TO REPRESENT HUNTINGDON AT THE NEXT GENERAL ELECTION. HE WOULD HAVE TO WAIT FOUR LONG YEARS BEFORE THE ELECTION WAS CALLED IN 1979. JOHN FOUGHT THE SEAT AS THOUGH HIS LIFE DEPENDED ON IT - WHICH IT DID. HE WON BY NEARLY 23,000 VOTES.

I, THE RETURNING OFFICER, HEREBY DECLARE ... OH, BUGGER. SORRY, EVERYONE; MAJOR'S WON.

AND SO, AFTER YEARS OF GNOME MAKING, BANKING IN NIGERIA, AND BUILDING SKY-SCRAPERS THAT NO ONE WANTED, JOHN FINALLY ENTERED PARLIAMENT. BY ALL ACCOUNTS HIS MAIDEN SPEECH WAS A FAIRLY FEATURELESS EFFORT - LITTLE MORE THAN A FAWNING APPROVAL OF GEOFFREY HOWE'S TRAGIC FIRST BUDGET.

WITH THE BEST WILL IN THE WORLD THE CHANCELLOR'S JOB IS NOT AN EASY ONE. OH NO. IN ORDER TO CREATE JOBS AND MAINTAIN PUBLIC SERVICES IT IS NECESSARY TO CUT PUBLIC SERVICES AND CREATE UNEMPLOYMENT.

DREARY AS IT WAS, HIS PERFORMANCE DID NOT GO UNNOTICED. HIGH IN A BELFRY ABOVE THE PALACE OF WESTMINSTER HE WAS BEING WATCHED.

CECIL. THAT MAN DOWN THERE HAS CAUGHT OUR EYE. IS HE ONE OF 'US'? OR IS HE ONE OF 'THEM'?

INDUBITABLY ONE OF 'US', MAJESTY. HIS NAME'S MAJOR. ONE OF THE NEW INTAKE.

JOHN DIDN'T REALISE IT, BUT HIS POLITICAL CAREER WAS BEGINNING ITS METEORIC ASCENT.

WE WANT HIM NURTURED AND GROOMED IN OUR OWN IMAGE, CECIL. WE WANT HIM READY FOR THE HIGHEST OFFICE WHEN THE FORCES OF DARKNESS COME FOR ME. AND, MARK MY WORDS, CECIL, COME FOR ME THEY WILL. THE TALL BLONDE ONE IS ONLY BIDING THE HOUR. INSTRUCT MAYHEW TO PROMOTE OUR MR. MAJOR TO THE WHIPS OFFICE.

YOUR WISH IS MY COMMAND, O GREAT ONE.

ALTHOUGH HE HADN'T BEEN IN PARLIAMENT VERY LONG, JOHN WAS BECOMING DEJECTED: ALL HIS COLLEAGUES WERE BEING RAPIDLY PROMOTED AND HE IMAGINED HE WAS BEING PASSED OVER. ACCORDING TO PENNY JUNOR, HE WAS TRULY GLUM.

I AM TRULY GLUM. OH YES.

THEN ONE DAY HE RECEIVED A CALL FROM THE CHIEF WHIP INVITING HIM TO BECOME A JUNIOR WHIP. HE WAS TREMENDOUSLY EXCITED.

I AM TREMENDOUSLY EXCITED. AND NOT INCONSIDERABLY SO.

JOHN IMMEDIATELY PHONED NORMA TO TELL HER THE GOOD NEWS. NORMA WAS THRILLED, ALTHOUGH SHE HAD NO IDEA WHAT A WHIP WAS OR DID.

HELLO NORMA. I'M A WHIP NOW. AND I'M ON THE FIRST RUNG OF THE LADDER. THAT IS TO SAY MY FOOT IS ON IT.

WHIP? BLADDER?

IT'S A BAD LINE, JOHN. DID YOU SAY YOU'VE PUT YOUR FOOT IN SOME DUNG? HAVE YOU GOT A PROBLEM WITH YOUR BLADDER?

NO. I'M IN A STATE OF TREMENDOUS EXCITEMENT. I THOUGHT YOU'D BE THRILLED.

I AM THRILLED.

I THOUGHT YOU WOULD BE.

THE JOB OF A WHIP IS TO FIND OUT IF BACK BENCHERS HAVE ANY NASTY LITTLE SECRETS, AND THEN THREATEN THEM WITH EXPOSURE IF THEY DON'T TOE THE PARTY LINE.

AH, JOHN. HAMILTON'S PLAYING HARD TO GET OVER WILLIE'S PAVING BILL. BE A GOOD FELLOW AND GO AND HAVE A LITTLE CHAT WITH HIM. SEE IF HE'S GOT ANY DIRT UNDER HIS FINGER-NAILS. DIRTY LINEN OR SKELETONS IN THE CUPBOARD. OK?

AND SO JOHN CONTINUED TO RISE AND RISE. AFTER A YEAR SPYING ON OTHERS IN THE DHSS, HE WAS PROMOTED AGAIN. THIS TIME TO THE POST OF CHIEF SECRETARY TO THE TREASURY. ACCORDING TO PENNY JUNOR, JOHN SPENT TWO HAPPY YEARS THERE EATING CRISPS. BUT HE HATED THE WORK BECAUSE IT MADE HIM ILL. SOME OF HIS COLLEAGUES BECAME ALARMED.

CHRIST, JOHN! YOU DON'T LOOK AT ALL WELL. YOU'RE A GHASTLY GREY COLOUR!

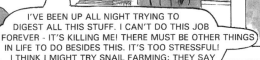

I'VE BEEN UP ALL NIGHT TRYING TO DIGEST ALL THIS STUFF. I CAN'T DO THIS JOB FOREVER - IT'S KILLING ME! THERE MUST BE OTHER THINGS IN LIFE TO DO BESIDES THIS. IT'S TOO STRESSFUL! I THINK I MIGHT TRY SNAIL FARMING; THEY SAY IT'S GOING TO BE THE GROWTH INDUSTRY OF THE FUTURE.

NIGEL LAWSON, WHO WAS CHANCELLOR AT THE TIME, REMEMBERS BECOMING CONCERNED THAT JOHN WASN'T UP TO THE JOB OF CHIEF SECRETARY.

NIGEL! THE ECONOMY'S OVER-HEATING! HOUSE PRICES ARE GOING THROUGH THE ROOF! ALL THE SECRETARIES OF STATE ARE BANGING ON MY DOOR BEGGING FOR MORE AND MORE MONEY FOR THEIR DEPARTMENTS. JOHN MOORE IS BEING HORRIBLE TO ME...

CHOMP! GUZZLE! BURP!

AND THERE WERE PROBLEMS AT HOME. JOHN AND NORMA HAD RECENTLY PURCHASED A HOUSE IN A VILLAGE NEAR HUNTINGDON. NORMA SPENT ALL HER TIME THERE WHILE JOHN STAYED IN LONDON.

THE GARDEN'S OVER-RUN WITH RABBITS! THE HORRIBLE THINGS ARE BESIEGING THE HOUSE! I'VE TRIED SHOOTING THEM BUT I KEEP MISSING! YOU'VE GOT TO COME HOME, JOHN. I CAN'T COPE!

I'M A BIT BUSY JUST NOW, DEAR. NIGEL'S GONE OUT TO LUNCH AGAIN AND ISN'T DUE BACK IN THE OFFICE UNTIL TOMORROW WHEN HE'S GOT ANOTHER BIG LUNCH TO ATTEND. I WONDER IF THESE RABBITS ARE ANGORAN RABBITS?

OH, FOR CHRIST'S SAKE STOP MOANING, MAN! THE ECONOMY'S FINE! LET IT RIP, I SAY. WE'VE GOT AN ELECTION COMING UP, SO LET THE LUMPEN MASSES THINK THEIR BEASTLY LITTLE HOVELS ARE SUDDENLY WORTH A FORTUNE IF IT MAKES THEM FEEL GOOD. ANYWAY, I'VE GOT A RATHER GOOD LUNCH COMING UP IN THE CITY IN HALF AN HOUR. SO, IF YOU WOULDN'T MIND HOLDING THE FORT FOR A DAY OR SO.

IN JUNE OF 1987 A GENERAL ELECTION WAS HELD. THE CONSERVATIVE PARTY WON EASILY. BUT IT WAS TO BE MARGARET THATCHER'S LAST VICTORY. IT WAS BEGINNING TO DAWN ON SOME WITHIN THE PARTY, AND TO LARGE SECTIONS OF THE BRITISH PUBLIC, THAT WHILE WHAT WAS KNOWN AS 'THATCHERISM' HAD SERVED ITS PURPOSE, MARGARET THATCHER HERSELF WAS AN IRREDEEMABLY HORRIBLE OLD BITCH WHO NEEDED TO HAVE A STAKE DRIVEN THROUGH HER HEART. MRS. THATCHER WAS AWARE OF THESE RUMBLINGS OF DISCONTENT AND EMBARKED ON A SUICIDAL RESHUFFLE OF HER CABINET. SHE HAD PLANNED THAT CECIL PARKINSON - WHO SHE'D CALLED 'THE SON SHE WISHED SHE'D HAD'- WOULD REPLACE HER WHEN THE MEN IN WHITE COATS CAME. BUT CECIL HAD BEEN OBLIGED TO RESIGN FROM THE CABINET YEARS EARLIER FOLLOWING THE REVELATION THAT HE WAS A SMARMY OLD CAD WHO HAD FATHERED A CHILD BY HIS SECRETARY. SHE HAD SAID AT THE TIME: 'THERE'S ONLY ONE PERSON I WANT TO SEE SUCCEED ME, NOW THAT CECIL'S GONE, JOHN MAJOR'. MARGARET THATCHER HAD LONG VIEWED HER FOREIGN SECRETARY, SIR GEOFFREY HOWE, WITH DEEP SUSPICION, BELIEVING HIM TO BE A 'WET' AND FAR TOO FOND OF THE GOOD LIFE THAT GOES WITH THE JOB. SHE ALSO HATED SIR GEOFFREY'S WIFE, ELSPETH. LATE ON MONDAY 24 JULY SHE SUMMONED JOHN MAJOR TO THE BELFRY.

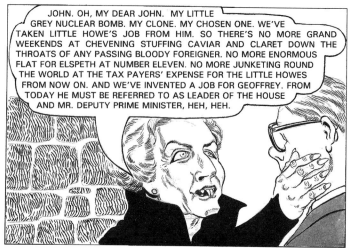

JOHN. OH, MY DEAR JOHN. MY LITTLE GREY NUCLEAR BOMB. MY CLONE. MY CHOSEN ONE. WE'VE TAKEN LITTLE HOWE'S JOB FROM HIM. SO THERE'S NO MORE GRAND WEEKENDS AT CHEVENING STUFFING CAVIAR AND CLARET DOWN THE THROATS OF ANY PASSING BLOODY FOREIGNER. NO MORE ENORMOUS FLAT FOR ELSPETH AT NUMBER ELEVEN. NO MORE JUNKETING ROUND THE WORLD AT THE TAX PAYERS' EXPENSE FOR THE LITTLE HOWES FROM NOW ON. AND WE'VE INVENTED A JOB FOR GEOFFREY. FROM TODAY HE MUST BE REFERRED TO AS LEADER OF THE HOUSE AND MR. DEPUTY PRIME MINISTER, HEH, HEH.

YOU ARE MY NEW FOREIGN SECRETARY NOW, JOHN. BUT YOU'RE NOT GOING TO BE IN THAT JOB FOR LONG. NO, YOU'RE GOING TO BE CHANCELLOR OF MY EXCHEQUER. MY FRIEND, ALAN WALTERS, WANTED ME TO GET RID OF LAWSON IN THIS RESHUFFLE. BUT IT WOULDN'T LOOK GOOD IF WE SACKED TWO MINISTERS IN ONE DAY. SO WE ARE KEEPING THE BLOATED LAWSON WHERE HE IS FOR THE TIME BEING. YOU SEE, MY PERFECT CREATION, I WANT YOU TO SUCCEED ME WHEN THE TIME COMES.

AND SO JOHN MOVED TO THE FOREIGN OFFICE. HIS WAS NOT A POPULAR APPOINTMENT WITH THE 'MANDARINS' WHO INHABITED THE CORRIDORS OF WHITEHALL.

MAJOR! I DON'T SUPPOSE THE BUGGER'S EVEN GOT A PASSPORT!

DON'T THINK CREATURES FROM HIS SORT OF BACKGROUND ARE GRANTED PASSPORTS, OLD MAN.

JOHN WAS ONLY AT THE FOREIGN OFFICE FOR THREE MONTHS. BUT HE LEARNED A GREAT DEAL THERE.

NOW REPEAT AFTER ME: KABUL IS THE CAPITAL OF AFGHANISTAN. TIRANA IS THE CAPITAL OF ALBANIA. ARABIA COMPRISES OF MANY STATES SOME OF WHICH ARE CALLED SHEIKDOMS AND ARE RULED BY SHEIKS. WE ARE NICE TO SHEIKS BECAUSE THEY HAVE LOTS OF·OIL AND MONEY. BUT WE DON'T LIKE OR APPROVE OF THEM, OR THEIR DISGUSTING HABITS.

ONCE AGAIN, JOHN RECEIVED A CALL FROM THE BELFRY.

GET UP HERE NOW!

ER...I'M A LITTLE TIED UP JUST NOW, I'M AFRAID, PRIME MINISTER.

I SAID NOW!

MEANWHILE NIGEL LAWSON'S POSITION WAS BEING CLEVERLY UNDERMINED BY MRS THATCHER AND A RATHER PECULIAR LITTLE MAN CALLED ALAN WALTERS WHO ADVISED THE PRIME MINISTER ON ECONOMIC MATTERS AND REFERRED TO LAWSON'S POLICIES AS 'HALF-BAKED'. LAWSON COULD TAKE THESE HUMILIATIONS NO LONGER AND RESIGNED THE CHANCELLORSHIP ON 26 OCTOBER. AGAIN JOHN WAS SUMMONED TO THE BELFRY AND WAS GIVEN THE POSITION OF CHANCELLOR. IT WAS A JOB JOHN HAD ALWAYS WANTED. MARGARET THATCHER, BELIEVING SHE HAD CONSIGNED LAWSON AND HOWE TO THE DUSTBIN OF POLITICAL HISTORY, NOW FELT HER PRIME MINISTERSHIP TO BE SECURE. SHE COULD NOT HAVE BEEN MORE WRONG. HARBOURING A DEEP GRUDGE, SIR GEOFFREY HOWE WAS PLOTTING HIS REVENGE. IN OCTOBER 1990 SIR GEOFFREY RESIGNED FROM HIS NON-EXISTENT JOB IN ORDER TO DELIVER A SPEECH - RUMOURED TO HAVE BEEN WRITTEN BY HIS WIFE - THAT WOULD IRREPARABLY DAMAGE HER PREMIERSHIP. WAITING IN THE WINGS AS THE DRAMA UNFOLDED WAS MICHAEL HESELTINE. HE HAD BEEN BIDING HIS TIME SINCE FLOUNCING OUT OF THE CABINET IN A HUFF IN 1986. HE HAD LONG HELD THE VIEW THAT BECAUSE HE WAS TALL, HAD LOTS OF HAIR AND MONEY, AND AN OVERWEENING SENSE OF HIS OWN IMPORTANCE, HE SHOULD NATURALLY BE PREMIER. HE ANNOUNCED HIS INTENTION TO STAND AGAINST MARGARET THATCHER IN A LEADERSHIP CONTEST.

WE INTEND TO FIGHT THE BLOND USURPER, MY GRANITE-HUED PROTEGE. HURD WILL PROPOSE ME, AND YOU WILL SECOND HIS PROPOSAL. IF WE FAIL AT THE FIRST BALLOT, TOFFEE-NOSE HURD WILL WANT TO STAND. HE DOESN'T STAND A CHANCE AGAINST THAT TRAITOR HESELTINE. SO WE ARE CALLING IN OUR DEBTS, MAJOR, AND YOU ARE DEEPLY IN DEBT, AREN'T YOU? IF WE GO DOWN THEN YOU ARE TO STAND AGAINST HESELTINE. DO WE MAKE OUR-SELF CLEAR?

OH YES.

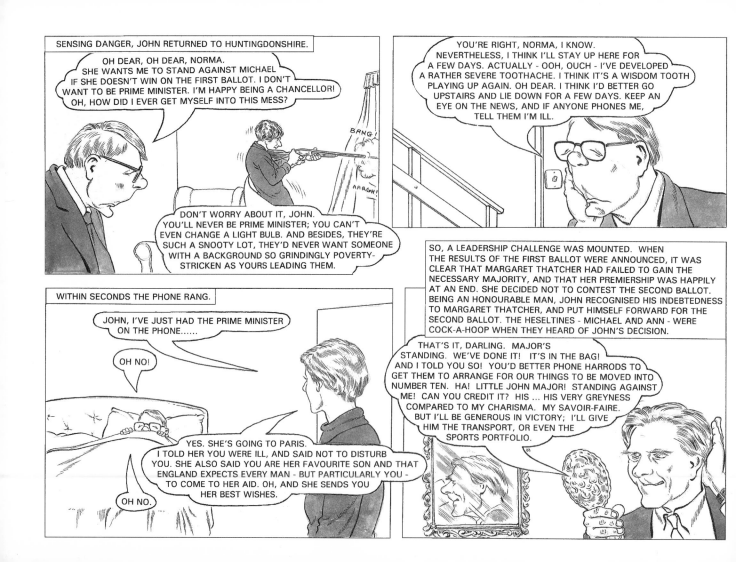

BUT HESELTINE HAD NOT RECKONED ON A SIGNIFICANT NUMBER OF TORY MPs WHO BELIEVED THAT, BY VOTING FOR JOHN IN THE SECOND BALLOT, THEY WOULD BE VOTING FOR A MORE ACCEPTABLE FORM OF THATCHERITE PHILOSOPHY: THATCHERISM WITHOUT THATCHER. THE RESULTS OF THE SECOND BALLOT WERE; HESELTINE, 131. HURD, PRACTICALLY NONE. JOHN MAJOR, 185. JOHN HAD WON. JOHN MAJOR WAS NOW THE PRIME MINISTER. MICHAEL HESELTINE AND HIS WIFE CAME OUT OF THEIR BELGRAVIA MANSION TO GRACEFULLY CONCEDE DEFEAT. ANN HESELTINE LOOKED MORE THAN A LITTLE GOB-SMACKED.

I BESTOW MY FULSOME AND UNSWERVING SUPPORT ON JOHN MAJOR. I WILL GO FURTHER; I WILL AVOW TO FOLLOW HIM TO THE ENDS OF THE EARTH IN PURSUIT OF ... SOMETHING OR OTHER ...

I JUST DON'T BELIEVE IT! IT CAN'T BE POSSIBLE!

AND THAT, GENTLE READER, IS MORE OR LESS THE END OF THE STORY. EXCEPT, THAT IS, FOR TERRY MAJOR. WHILE JOHN WENT ON TO BECOME EVEN LESS POPULAR THAN MARGARET THATCHER, TERRY CARVED OUT A NEW CAREER AS A TELEVISION PERSONALITY, A NOTED AUTHORITY ON GARDEN GNOMES AND CROYDON'S ELECTRICITY SUPPLY, AND A CONNOISSEUR OF BEAUTIFUL WOMEN. OH, AND HE ALSO HAS WRITTEN A WONDERFUL MEMOIR OF HIS BROTHER CALLED 'MAJOR MAJOR' WHICH HAS BEEN THE INSPIRATION FOR THIS BOOK.

THE END

SHORTY AFTERWARDS JOHN MAJOR ARRIVED OUTSIDE NUMBER TEN DOWNING STREET.

I'M GOING IN THERE NOW TO DO MY BUSINESS. I MAY BE GONE A LONG TIME. BUT, THEN AGAIN I MAY ONLY BE GONE A SHORT WHILE ... ER ...

Epilogue

Since the completion of this book, John's sister, Patricia, has appeared as a personality in her own right in the pages of *The Daily Telegraph*. Patricia Major-Ball's life is little documented in the two books I've used as sources for my own book. Consequently, there is only one mention of her in this biography.

However, it is now clear that Patricia played a pivotal role in the life and times of John Major. Ownership of the Angoran rabbit referred to on page 10 is now a matter of dispute. Patricia claims that, as she was obliged to sweep up its copious droppings, the rabbit must have belonged to her. She further claims there was considerable friction between Jean Collins and herself over who should wash John's clothes.

Much about Patricia Major-Ball can be gleaned from the fact that she spent many years designing the insides of cigarette lighters for Ronson lighters, and from her acknowledged aim in life 'to help British women find a middle path through their underwear drawer'.